"In reading Susan Swartz's wonderful *Juicy Tomatoes Guide to Ripe Living After 50,* I laughed out loud, recognizing so many of my own internalized myths about the aging process. What a relief to realize that there are so many gutsy and brave women over fifty who have turned life's detours and challenges into grand opportunities through their amazing resourcefulness and creativity. These passionate and daring risk takers are a joyful testimony to the new possibilities of womanhood. The lives of so-called "ordinary women" are woven into the most extraordinary tapestry of good advice and celebration of joyful living. Resonating throughout every story is the profoundness of Eleanor Roosevelt's message, "You must do the thing you think you cannot do.""

—*Molly Murphy MacGregor, executive director and the cofounder of*
the *National Women's History Project*

"After reading this second book by Susan, I've realized that not only am I juicy AND ripe, I've been marinating long enough! No more excuses! I'm gonna get out there and LIVE! I would be happy to call any one of the women in this book, 'Sister.' Susan knows how to bring the 'juice' out of each of us!"

—*Dee Adams, creator of* Minnie Pauz

"The *Juicy Tomatoes Guide to Ripe Living After 50* gives you a girl's night out without leaving your favorite reading chair—or bubble bath. It's a "whew!" for those of us at 50+ who have thoughts 180 degrees different from our mothers, letting us know we aren't alone. And a nudge down a path we were contemplating but needed just a bit more courage to take the first step."

—*Jeanie Linders, writer and producer of* Menopause: The Musical,
founder of Aging Out Loud, and publisher of W4W VOICES

the juicy tomatoes guide to

Ripe living after 50

susan swartz

New Harbinger Publications, Inc.

Publisher's Note

This publication is designed to provide accurate and authoritative information in regard to the subject matter covered. It is sold with the understanding that the publisher is not engaged in rendering psychological, financial, legal, or other professional services. If expert assistance or counseling is needed, the services of a competent professional should be sought.

Distributed in Canada by Raincoast Books.

Copyright © 2006 by Susan Swartz
New Harbinger Publications, Inc.
5674 Shattuck Avenue
Oakland, CA 94609
www.newharbinger.com

Cover and text design by Amy Shoup; Cover illustration by Shannon Laskey/www.smalldogworkshop.com
Acquired by Melissa Kirk; Edited by Karen Stein

Library of Congress Cataloging-in-Publication Data

Swartz, Susan.
  The juicy tomatoes guide to ripe living after 50 / Susan Swartz.
      p. cm.
  ISBN 1-57224-432-1
  1. Middle-aged women--United States--Life skills guides. I. Title.
  HQ1059.5.U5S93 2006
  305.244'2--dc22
                                      2005037407

08 07 06

10   9   8   7   6   5   4   3   2   1

First printing

For my three daughters

Contents

Acknowledgments

Thanks to the creative brains around the table at New Harbinger Publications. And to the amazing women who agreed to share their stories, including my always-generous friends.

Thanks to my newspaper, the Santa Rosa Press Democrat, which gives me a voice, and to the New York Times News Service, which sends it around the country.

Thanks to Teresa Meikle for her sound research. And to my funny, loving family, especially Klose, the best editor.

Introduction

With all the talk about a longevity revolution and fifty being the new thirty (and, I suppose, eighty soon becoming the new sixty), getting older has never seemed so young. Juicy Tomatoes already know this.

Juicy Tomatoes is my term for certain women who are full, ripe, luscious, still on the vine, and past the half-century mark. Even before official sources recognized the changing habits and expectations of people at midlife and beyond, Tomatoes were setting an example.

Now we have the U.S. Census Bureau and other numbers people declaring that Americans are living and working longer, skiing and having babies later than ever, and indulging themselves with cosmetic peels and river rafting trips with their grandkids.

American women now have a life expectancy of just over 80 years (actually 80.1), an all-time high. The challenge is to make those 80.1 active, conscious, curious years. For that we need to start practicing right now.

Thanks to the baby boomers, the number of women over fifty continues to swell faster than a forehead on Botox. The time is ripe. If we're going to improve the image of aging, it needs to happen now. That's why when someone reports news about midlife women, I take notes. I collect stories about women of a certain age. I hang out with them. I interview them for my newspaper column. I whoop and holler when I see them portrayed honestly in books and the movies. Credible and funny, smart and thoughtful, they wear their maturity with panache. Oh, sure, they grouse about their brown spots and brain glitches and maybe they have a few regrets about the road not taken, but they're not paralyzed by birthday numbers.

There are 44 million American women age fifty and over. They make up 15 percent of the population. They have a lot to say, which is why I keep writing about them.

My first book on the subject, *Juicy Tomatoes: Plain Truths, Dumb Lies, and Sisterly Advice About Life After 50,* looked at the stereotypes of invisible, predictable middle age and how women were discovering there is more to midlife than menopause, empty nests, and trying to relive their younger years.

Working on that book I met a robust, healthy pack of determined fifty-somethings, and while doing readings around the country I met even more. They had a confidence and attitude that surprised me. They weren't whining about getting older—they were taking risks, going back to school, exploring new religions, saving trees, moving to another country.

They inspired me to write *The Juicy Tomatoes Guide to Ripe Living after 50,* with its practical advice and true-life examples of women who are continuing the adventure. Some names you'll recognize and some you won't, but you might want to call them if you're ever in their town.

The first book established that aging is full of many challenges. What are those lines around my neck? Will I ever have sex again? Can a person die from hot flashes?

This book doesn't dismiss those worries but goes beyond. Here are women who have figured out what they want or need to do next. They have made some pretty interesting discoveries about themselves in their fifties, sixties, and beyond. Isabel Allende says age has given her power.

"I've become a witch," she says. A Midwestern banker says continued passion for her job gives her reason "to put my pantyhose on every morning."

I continued the Juicy Tomatoes moniker because women say it fits. After reading my first book, a hiking group who used to call themselves "Buzzard Bait Broads" renamed themselves the "Juicy Tomatoes." So did a group of women who retreat to a beach house once a year.

We're not alone in our need for encouragement. Women of other cultures apparently share the same issues. My first *Juicy Tomatoes* book has been translated into Greek, Korean, Portuguese, and German. The German version has its own title that translates to "Old Am Still for a Long Time Not I."

That's true. We have a long way to go. In fact, scientists are now saying that we should be planning for our extended longevity—that instead of measuring aging by how long a person has lived, it makes more sense to consider how many years she can still look forward to. Welcome aboard. This is the spin we were looking for: that there's more to come, lots to do.

If you think of it that way, then you want to make every decade stand out so you get to experience what Gloria Steinem calls "the roominess of life." Claim this time, this age. Make it different from anything you've done before. Then you can say, "In my fifties I went to China and took up the trombone." Or "That was the decade I had breast cancer and lived and ran my first 10K." "When I became a grandmother and ran for the school board." "When I got the braces off my teeth and had my last baby."

Allow me to take one paragraph for myself to report that my own fifties were full of firsts. My husband and I got to live in Europe for two years. I learned a little bit of German. I flew over Sarajevo to drop war-relief food packages. I took improvisational acting. I started doing radio commentary. My book was turned into a play. I went on TV covered with so much makeup that I looked like a Geisha madam. I finally found some pills that work on migraines. I started going

3

to baseball games. I took beginning French. And get this: the *Oxford English Dictionary* credited me with coming up with the term "bad hair day." When we meet, I'll tell you about it.

Suffice it to say, Tomatoes understand about bad hair days. We have our noble and world-saving goals and don't let the petty stuff get to us, but that doesn't mean we don't have vanity issues. You'll be reading about my ninety-five-year-old therapist friend who takes forty minutes getting dressed in the morning, because no one but the cat gets to see her without makeup on and earrings in place.

This book is full of real women. Some are friends. Some are celebrities. Many are everyday women I've met through my newspaper work and by asking around for women with great stories to tell. Some are identified by first name only. A few chose pseudonyms, but surprisingly most of them used their real names, even when discussing the most intimate subjects. I've tried to present positive role models, but that doesn't mean I avoided the difficult realities of getting older. People talk about this decade as the "fatal fifties" because this is a period when we realize that something is going to get us. Not everyone is going to get to live her entitled 80.1 years. Several of the women in this book made big changes because someone close to them died.

But Tomatoes are hardy. They don't require a lot of pampering. A little encouragement and they deliver, even in bad dirt. The riper they get the better they taste. And if you add a bit of salt they really come alive.

PART ONE

Discovering
Your Juice

What Is a Juicy Tomato?

S he's a woman of indeterminate age—not old, not young, but somewhere in the middle. She has a proud walk, a breezy glamour, a piece of amber hanging from her throat, matching the gold glints in her hair. She has a small smile, from a secret amusement or memory. She is the picture of poise, until she lets it rip for her favorite basketball team.

Here's another. She has a shiny black braid, threaded with white. Her face is as open as her resolve is firm, as she circulates a ballot petition outside the grocery store. She has a firm handshake and she looks you in the eye. Would you guess that her younger self stared at her feet and thought she had nothing important to say?

Another is in a classic suit with black hose, heels, and a blondish bob, telling the leader of the free world, or the chairman of the board, that perhaps there's a different approach.

One more. She is strong and sleek in a body that could be called "zaftig." She's solid, like one of those goddess statues, but watch her twist that body into a backbend or flip up into the perfect headstand, a perch from which she will suggest that we all take a moment to focus on the here and now.

How could the world have ever ignored such women, suggesting that they were done because they had arrived at a birthday with a big "0" at the end and were no longer a foxy chick?

These are the pictures we hold in our heads on the days when we worry about becoming invisible and unnecessary. These women know what they've got. This does not mean that they don't also have days when they'd rather hide under the covers. Or when they look into their mirror and think, "Oh dear, what now?"

Each one has been bruised, some more than others. How could you not be a little dinged up after living half a century? They know that there are more bumps coming. They may wish they could redo some of those years—taken the risk, gone with the other man, pushed for a better position, majored in economics. But mostly they've stopped trying to measure up to someone else's idea of success. They know who they are and that's pretty good.

They are like Millie, who plans to get a navel ring for her sixtieth birthday, a reward for herself for all those years of working out. Hang around these women. Ask them what books they read, what vitamins they take, where they get their juice.

Once there was an accepted notion, which we now know is a myth, that women naturally fade with age. Don't buy into it. A lot of women become more visible in these middle years. I know a woman named Michele who does a rock-and-roll show on public radio, dresses in animal prints, and colors her hair pomegranate. She admits that she was a shy young girl. She looks at herself not as growing older but as growing stronger, and she reports that this new ability "to speak in public and on the radio and to be comfortable in my own skin is quite delightful. At times I sparkle and I can feel that." She adds that she's a "more effective flirt today than I ever was before."

At midlife women are not as cautious as their younger, self-conscious selves. You see them in improvisational acting classes, leading a teachers' strike, running for office against younger men. We're everywhere.

Next time you see an outgoing older woman, ask her if she was always this confident and daring. Chances are she'll say, "God, no. I constantly surprise myself."

Are We Okay with This?

It's essential to have peers to whom you can say, "Tell me again, what do we like about being older?" If you're lucky you will get your friend on an up day when she has something positive to report. Her encouragement can remind you that this is the time of living when we work on what we can and let the rest go—or at least not be whining all the time about what you should have or could have done.

The fifties are pivotal. They can be a downer, a stagnant place, or an interesting development. To ensure it's the latter, we need companions—hormonally and chronologically compatible friends and role models.

Kate says, "I think after fifty you finally pay attention to what you have in life. I'm not exactly doing what I want right now, or thought I would be doing at this age, but I can be peaceful about it." Kate gave herself a fifty-ninth birthday party and invited everyone from grade-school friends to colleagues in the public relations business. During the next ten years she intends to become a full-time writer, taking time

HOW TO TELL A JUICY TOMATO

- She flaunts her ripeness.

- She has a certain heft that comes from living full and long.

- Her soft spots are surprisingly sweet.

- All the little green tomatoes want to grow up to be like her.

- She looks forward to many saucy years ahead.

- And to one day becoming an heirloom tomato.

YOU TALKING TO ME?

We all have those first realizations that we have crossed over from the land of the young. What was your first sign?

- When the new guy in the office asked how many grandchildren you have.

- When the grocery store bagger, the waiter, the FedEx person called you "ma'am."

- When the flight attendant called you "love."

- When you started keeping tweezers in your car, and not to pluck your eyebrows.

- When you realized that you have a new neck, and it's old.

- When a colleague described you as venerable.

- When your sister-in-law asked if you've thought of having work done, and she didn't mean a bathroom remodel.

- When you went to a family wedding and your cousin's kids went out back to get high and didn't invite you.

out for ski vacations in France. How that will happen she's not sure, but she says her stepmother made huge changes in her life, going to art school in her late fifties and meeting and marrying the love of her life, so Kate's sure she can do it, too.

Pam talks about an old family friend named Fran who is one of her models for getting older. "Fran had been friends with Margaret Mead. She had a huge, roaring laugh and was about six feet two and was old, at least middle age, by the time I knew her. Fran had also known Carl Jung. She said he told her you have to laugh loud every day to be healthy. She was a gracious woman and represented for me the potential of intellectual endeavor. I always wanted to be like Fran when I got older."

Usually in your fifties the nest starts to empty. You no longer work around playdates and soccer games, unless you're one of those middle-aged mommies we'll talk about later. There's a new freedom to mourn or indulge. Leslie, after raising three sons on her own and packing the youngest one off to college, figured out a way to fill her weekends so she wouldn't dread Friday nights in an empty house, and set about positioning herself to go teach abroad.

Pam, a watercolor artist, swears she's more productive than ever with her two sons away at school, husband at work in a separate studio, and aging dog that is less demanding than before. "I've become a workaholic for the first time in my life," she says. Every morning at seven she takes her cup of tea to the studio behind her house, builds a fire in the woodstove and starts to paint. While she works she listens to opera lectures on tape and Terry Gross on NPR. She's generating more artwork and sales than ever.

This is the time in life when you start to figure out a balance, says Neva, who chairs an opera committee, sits on the board of a community foundation, and is turning the garage from a family dumping ground into her private studio.

"This is what I want to do now," says Neva. "Paint, contribute to my community, be with my family, play with my grandbabies, meditate, and take time to boogie."

Media: Friend or Foe?

Even if the movie *Something's Gotta Give* hadn't been a box office hit, Diane Keaton would have deserved a special award for appearing in front of a camera without reconstruction. God knows, we welcome any message that says it's okay to be who we are.

How the mass media presents our age group has a lot to do with our own self-esteem, even if we're no Diane Keaton and it's only a fantasy movie. A woman in her late fifties who is fit and smart and having sex with Jack Nicholson and Keanu Reeves and not dying in the end from a terminal disease earns big points from our crowd.

In the past, middle-aged female characters were either ignored, mocked, or turned into desperate, loony types. So, we take note of any encouraging signs from Hollywood and other media that show us what our culture thinks of us.

At fifty-seven Charlotte Rampling was chosen by hip designer Marc Jacobs to appear in an ad campaign. And at fifty-three Anjelica Huston modeled for Harry Winston. Here's Anjelica, wearing diamonds over her tank top, her dark hair framing that wise face, sporting a playful smile and honest-to-goodness laugh lines. Compare that to Lauren Hutton being told in 1984, when she was forty, that she was no longer needed for Revlon's ads. Fast forward to Lauren Hutton returning as a cosmetic entrepreneur and becoming pretty much the mature woman's cover girl.

Jamie Lee Curtis had women cheering when she posed in her undies and real flesh for *More* magazine, revealing that even Hollywood stars have cellulite peeking out from under their bicycle shorts. At the time Jamie was a relatively young forty-three, but women of all ages made her their reality hero.

Even if we're in a different league from these famous women, it helps the greater cause when a movie reviewer says that Susan Sarandon, at fifty-eight, is way too hot to play a neglected wife. And it doesn't hurt when Joel Selvin, writer for the *San Francisco Chronicle* says of Rita Moreno, "She strutted, she cooed. She sang with a sexy twinkle in her smile. She walked with a sultry twitch in her stride. She belted and she whispered. At age seventy-three she looked better than most women half her age."

That doesn't mean that the mass media has finally come to admire and respect older women for their full lives and natural beauty. You still see ads for antiaging products that say something like, "You can be saggy and baggy, or you can look like this stunning air-brushed model if you buy our $50 miracle cream," or remind you to get your Botox before the Christmas parties start.

But marketers now know to pitch to boomer women, says San Francisco advertising executive Millie Olson. For a collagen beauty product, her Amazon Advertising agency came up with an ad with a woman saying, "My friends and I said we wouldn't worry about aging, and then I found out they were cheating." The tagline says, "Age gracefully. Later." The idea behind that, says Millie, is that "we will bear and accept getting older with some grace but we'll deal with what we can." It also recognized that "women respond to realistic humor."

Still, she says, it's a tricky balance to present both realistic and attractive models to speak to the age group. "Boomers want to have it both ways. We want to be represented by people we can relate to but who don't make us feel old." In one instance she had difficulty finding models "who were over forty and realistic looking." In other instances she has avoided using gray-haired models. "Some women say that even if they choose to leave their own hair gray, they don't want to see gray hair in an ad."

For another ad campaign Millie organized a focus group of middle-aged women and asked them to talk about their sexuality. "Certainly they talked about the enjoyment of having sex, but it went deeper. To them sexuality was about self-image and vitality—how you feel when you're walking down the street with your hair swinging. It's a feeling women don't want to give up."

A boomer herself, Millie personally identifies with the market and is encouraged that advertisers are becoming more sensitive. "For one thing, boomers will insist on staying the center of attention. None of us is ready to leave the stage yet. I assume we'll change the rules as we go."

Advertising messages sell more than a product. They can change—or support—an unflattering stereotype, like the Super Bowl beer ad that showed young guys talking about how young women turn into their mothers. The big hoot comes when the camera flashes on a middle-aged mother with a pretty face and then drops to show her clownlike behind.

But how about the Dove soap campaign that tried to educate the public on a broader vision of beauty? Billboards showed the face of a vivacious gray-haired woman with the words "Graying or gorgeous?" Another pictured a ninety-five-year-old and asked, "Wrinkled or wonderful?" The billboard campaign followed the company's study of three thousand women in ten countries who were asked to talk about beauty. Only 2 percent considered themselves beautiful by the culture's standards, but, happily, more than 80 percent believed that a woman can be beautiful at any age.

Many fashion catalogs now use the occasional white-haired model. It's true that they're slimmer and more gorgeous than you'll ever be. But they are not young.

TOP TEN WAYS TO STAY COOL OVER FIFTY

1. Even if you can't get to New York or Paris, check out the nearest hip neighborhood in your city. Hang out, observe, soak up the look.

2. Choose your trends wisely. Just because polka dots are "in" doesn't require you to wear them all over your torso. Maybe just on a belt or an eyeglass case.

3. Wear no clothing with embroidered words that identify you as the wife, the mom, or the grandma. Except around the Christmas tree.

4. Don't even try pop lingo unless you have a teenager in the house.

5. Be wary of retro. It's the look that's supposed to be retro, not you.

We even get the occasional upbeat coverage. The *New York Times* published a story on middle-aged snowboarders and called them "grays on trays." *Esquire* did an intelligent and admiring piece on the aging process in women. In *Doonesbury*, Joanie Caucus admitted she was retirement age and wasn't banished from the comic strip.

The advertising world still courts the eighteen-to-thirty-five market, because that age group is considered more apt to change brands. The belief is that brand preferences are established early and don't change as much as people age. But boomers aren't like their parents. They don't stay Ford people forever, any more than they'll stick with AT&T if Sprint gives them a better deal.

People between the ages of thirty-five and sixty-four are responsible for nearly two-thirds of consumer spending. Women in general make up to 80 percent of all purchasing decisions, from booze to blue jeans. The smart advertiser, you would think, would do as much as possible to court, or even suck up to, this huge market, by following the money and coming after us with ads that flatter our style and consumer savvy.

"Life shrinks or expands in proportion to one's courage."
—anaïs nin

The Hipness Factor

Can you be hip over fifty? How about cool? Is it cool to even use the words *cool* and *hip* anymore? If so, are we allowed to use the words after a certain age? And can they possibly still pertain to us?

Enough young people use the words *cool* and *hip* that they have more validity than, say, *groovy* or *neato*. But young people traditionally establish what is cool. There are sleuths called "cool hunters" who are dispatched to major cities to be the young eyes for marketing experts and report back on the latest in fashion and music, diets, the newest bar scene. They declare what's about to be "in," and we follow. A fifty-year-old may double-pierce, but she wasn't the one to make it cool in the first place.

Hipness is defined as being in touch with the fundamental cultural forces changing society, which means you don't necessarily have to start a cultural force to be hip. Or even participate in it. You can merely recognize it.

My friend Joanie, who reports on the ad business, points out that people over fifty do not have to set trends to enjoy them. "There are two ways to be hip," she says. "You either follow the pop culture or you influence it."

People in their thirties are going to be hipper because young people like to follow the buzz and everything is

6. Indulge the latest fashion in purses, scarves, and shoes. But don't buy those cute shoes if you can't walk in them. When a young woman trips in her high heels, it's charming. When anyone older does, people get nervous.

7. Learn and use the computer technology that most of the world uses to communicate.

8. If you don't get the *New Yorker* cartoons, it's probably a sign that you haven't been paying attention.

9. Don't brag too loud in the office about seeing the Beach Boys, but do mention the Lyle Lovett concert you attended.

10. Give it all a taste. Remember, you once thought sushi was disgusting.

new to them. They're not going to see rhinestone-studded eyeglass frames and think Aunt Bert and her mah-jongg friends like we might. They haven't been through two incarnations of shoulder pads and fun with fondue. The younger you are the more things look original.

Young people spend more energy and money in order to dress, eat, and enjoy what's hip. At least, that used to be the thinking. But the boomer consumer still has a stake in being hip and, unlike her parents' generation, does not necessarily feel she's outgrown pop culture. Linda is in a poetry group that often takes over a jazz bar for readings. She prefers that venue because it's got more style than a bookstore. "It makes me feel like I'm part of a scene, but not crashing it."

Being tuned in to the pop culture lets you into the conversation. "You can't be a fuddy-duddy and have a beer with a thirty-year-old," says Joanie. "But you can if you have enough common ground to have an exchange." Look around a music bar or coffeehouse and see how many people of your vintage are mixed in with the younger crowd. When there are enough people of your age group assembled at a so-called scene, "you become hip by default," says Joanie.

It's the effect of boomer bulge, she says. "There's so many of us, the young can't avoid us. It's not because we're so clever and hip. It's because we're such a large presence they have to pay attention."

You've Got to Have Friends

In our late forties, my husband and I moved to Germany so he could take a journalism job and I could be a hausfrau. My mission was to make one good woman friend while we were there. I ordered myself to be bold and outgoing and keep my antenna out for candidates.

I met Mary my first week there. She was an American, married to one of my husband's new colleagues, and she was wearing a "Take Back the Night" T-shirt. It was the T-shirt that did it.

I knew we were at least politically simpatico. But there was more. We both had daughters, older sisters, and husbands who were journalists, and we both missed NPR. We hung out in Germany, going to museums, taking a German language class, swapping books and CDs. We were like instant old pals, driving to Paris for a weekend, taking the train to Amsterdam. We talked about politics and women's issues and raising kids and whether she should put a Susan Sontag streak in her hair.

After six months, Mary moved back to the States, and my husband and I moved to another part of Germany, where I met Judy, also an American. She was sitting across from me at a meeting of the American Association of University Women in Munich, where we'd heard a report on the latest war casualties in the Balkans. After the speech Judy sighed and declared that what we needed to do was get all the women in the world to march into these battle zones and say, "Enough of this shit." I asked her if she'd like to go out for coffee.

Judy, a native of Washington DC, living in Germany, introduced me to some of Munich's best coffeehouses, along with beer gardens, bookstores, and theaters. Her husband and mine also clicked. Judy was a lot gutsier about using her German than I was, but she encouraged me to try, and one day I found myself able to report that I had made a German friend. I was in a drugstore, struggling to communicate my needs to a clerk, and another shopper offered to help. We started talking in a mix of German and English. It turned out that she'd spent her life in Munich but had studied one year in California. She asked if I drank coffee.

"If you have ever been called defiant, incorrigible, forward, cunning, insurgent, unruly, rebellious, you're on the right track."
—clarissa pinkola estés

How to Make the First Move

Kathryn recently moved to Arizona from North Carolina, although she's lived many places, from Europe to California. Being a book publicist and a single mother of a grown daughter, she can live pretty much wherever she wants, and she's an expert at making friends in new places. She usually gravitates toward churches, stores, art galleries, and yoga studios.

When she first got to the Phoenix area she joined an art studio tour, visited thirty-five studios in two weekends, and shook the hands and took the cards of one hundred artists. Figuring out the locations of all the studios helped her learn the neighborhood and started to make her feel more grounded in her community. "One woman invited me to lunch with another artist friend. I met a woman who was from my hometown in Utah who had a dog I fell in love with. I met a man with three German shepherds and asked him to recommend a local vet. My best treasure was a woman whose husband is a wonderful artist from Mexico. They own a small gallery and now I visit her every week."

When Kathryn lived in Asheville, North Carolina, she tried out thirteen different churches. At a Unitarian church she met Betsy, "one of those East Coast women who knows things like how to perfectly cook lobster, make crab cakes, and how long to cook the turkey. She and her husband came to my house for Thanksgiving and she stepped in at the perfect moment to make the gravy. We all need these kinds of women in our lives. She is the kind of friend who remembers you had that deadline or that houseguest or you were going to take a hike and always remembers to call and ask how it went."

Kathryn grew up in an Air Force family, so she's undaunted by a change of scenery. Her rule is to get to know as many neighbors as possible. "It's a basic recognition that we are all on the same planet and so living on the same street gives me license to ask people questions like 'What's your dog's name?' 'What day do we leave out the garbage?' 'Did you see that coyote?' 'Can you help me move this fence?'"

Having two dogs has helped her meet others. When she got to Cave Creek, near Phoenix, she started taking walks with other border collie owners and got involved in the local dog rescue program. Three months after moving to Arizona she gave herself a birthday party and invited the people she'd met so far and liked. Nineteen people came, mostly new neighbors and artists. Even though she works to cultivate her new friendships, she still spends an hour a day communicating with old friends by e-mail. "It's like what we learned in Girl Scouts. Make new friends, but the keep the old. One is silver, but the other is gold."

That Old Gang of Mine

Mary in Detroit has been part of two tight groups for close to twenty years: Her book group started out reading feminist authors and eventually broadened its focus. And her "poker" group, which has little to do with cards, meets for monthly dinners. She also belongs to a quilting group, a poetry writing group, and a Buddhist meditation group.

The book group was organized when one woman put an ad in an alternative newspaper saying she wanted to read feminist authors. Eight women showed, including Mary, and the membership has stayed pretty close to ten, as some have left the group and others have joined.

The poker group met each other at a women's justice center. "We were all real feminist and very politically active," says Mary, a lawyer. "We decided to see each other regularly and called it our 'poker club' as a joke, because that's what men do when they get together. But we didn't play it more than once." Mary was pregnant when both groups formed, so her now-college-age daughter grew up with two sets of her mother's friends. "We would meet at my house when she

Where can you find friends when you're new in town and don't regularly go to the spots where people commonly connect with others, like an office or the soccer mom's bench?

- **Gyms.** There is something about strangers running around half naked without makeup on that makes them open up to each other.

- **Choir practice.** Singers are naturally friendly because they need each other in order to sound good, and they always want new people for the carpool.

- **Book clubs.** Ask the staff at your local bookstore if they maintain a list of clubs looking for members. Some stores have them listed by genre—mystery, political nonfiction, women's fiction, Jane Austen.

was little because I was the only one with kids for a while. I'd be so tired from working they'd just take over and give her a bath and feed her while we talked about books and politics.

"I think my groups have lasted because there are no rules," says Mary. "You can still come to book club if you haven't read the book."

Get It Together

There are book groups, investment groups, writing groups, wine tasting groups, ethnic food groups, travel study groups, and support groups to sustain people through every shared loss and worry. But there are other ways to form a group. All you need is one imaginative woman and e-mail.

A jewelry artist named Jessica moved from a major city to a small town and wondered where the good jazz clubs were. Finding none, she started asking around to see who liked jazz and wanted to get together—not to play music, but to listen. She invited ten people to her house and each one brought one or two favorite CDs and selected a song from each. There was lots of food and wine consumption but no talking when the music was playing. After each piece, the person would explain what she knew about the musician and why she liked the tune, and then the next person would take her turn. Jessica called it a listening group and named it the Jazz Club. They became her new circle of friends.

Donna wanted to celebrate women's suffrage day, August 26, with a picnic at the beach. She invited a few friends and asked each of them to bring another friend. Donna provided the grilled salmon, and everyone else brought side dishes and drinks. Everyone raised their glasses to Elizabeth Cady Stanton, Susan B. Anthony, and all the good spirits who had helped women win the vote. Then the partygoers went around the circle to say what they had recently accomplished, perhaps a work promotion or getting a child through a bad drug period or surviving a health scare. When it got late and the fog rolled in, the women unrolled their sleeping bags and spent the night, and the next August they brought new friends.

Barbara, a writer and editor, inherited money from her brother and decided to publish a book of women's writings. She invited other writers in the area, some of whom she knew and some she didn't, to talk about her project one stormy January night over ravioli and chicken at an Italian restaurant. Barbara asked everyone who had something they were burning to see in print to submit a story for an anthology. They were invited to write "to their heart's content" about any subject. Their submissions would be edited, but no piece would be rejected. The women, who ranged in age from thirty to eighty, met through the spring and summer to read their pieces and

- **Local political headquarters.** No one is happier to welcome a new face than a committed group of exhausted idealists trying to push a ballot initiative to save the library or to canvass the neighborhood for their candidate. Start out by saying, "I can make signs and coffee and I'm really good at ringing doorbells."

- **Classrooms.** Language classes are good because everyone's feeling awkward together. You might even meet someone with a condo in Costa Rica.

- **Art openings.** Free wine, free food, and all ages share thoughts about the artwork with whoever's standing next to them.

- **Dog parks.** It's the same as it was when you were a young mother pushing your baby in a stroller. Dog people bond in the same way, cooing over each other's precious ones.

- **Your own network.** Before you move, ask your friends if they know anyone in Birmingham you can call to go out for coffee.

give each other feedback, eventually creating a book but also forming a writing community in the process. Barbara formed her own publishing company and met her deadline to publish in a year. When the book was printed, the women pooled their money and put on their dancing clothes for a raucous party at the community center.

A Juicy Bunch

During high school in the 1960s, Colleen and Cia worked at the same hamburger joint in Ukiah, California. Cia married Colleen's neighbor, a guy she had grown up with. Colleen moved out of town and came back fourteen years later, at which point she and Cia picked up where they had left off.

Judi, another Ukiah woman, was Colleen's son's high school running coach. When the two women met, they started exchanging books and soon found out they had much in common, including the fact that they "both like to eat cotton candy in the morning." Now Judi, Colleen, and Cia walk together every week. When they want to do a weekend away in Mendocino, a nearby coastal town, they add in Judi's sister Jennifer, Jennifer's friend Carol, Judi's friend Pat, Colleen's mother, and Cia's relative by marriage, Pauline. They call themselves the "Juicy Tomatoes" because one of them got my first book for a fiftieth birthday present, read it, and passed it on to another member, and so on. Indeed, theirs is a juicy agenda.

"When we get together we pamper ourselves, drink wine, have massages, shop, talk, and explore each other's lives," says Colleen. "We trade opinions, cook, and even made up a play about ourselves while crowded in a hot tub." Together they've dealt with cancer, an emergency appendectomy, kids leaving home, a son-in-law going to Iraq, aging parents, new houses. The group includes a nurse, a counselor, an interior designer, two teacher's assistants, one retiree, and a prison employee.

"We cry together, laugh together, keep keys to each other's houses. Our friendship is based on our differences as well as our similarities. We accept each other unconditionally," says Colleen, "and I don't believe any of us could ever move away, just because we couldn't be separated."

MYTH: This country's being overrun by young people.
FACT: Put in your lenses and look around. The number of people fifty-five and over equal the entire populations of New York, California, and Massachusetts combined. Thirty percent of American women are age fifty and over.

MYTH: I'll never have a baby now.
FACT: There were 1,512 first-time mothers between the ages of forty-five and fifty-four in 2003.

MYTH: I'll never marry again.
FACT: Get ready for hot flashes on your honeymoon. More than 75 percent of women in their fifties who are divorced enjoy a serious, exclusive relationship. Thirty-nine percent are remarried.

Then Came the Red Hats

Swarms of women in red hats and purple dresses have certainly solved the invisibility problem that once plagued older women. And the isolation, too. Members of the Red Hat Society dress to be seen, to demonstrate their goal to greet middle age and beyond with "verve, humor, and elan," in the words of its founder, Sue Ellen Cooper, a Fullerton, California, artist. She came up with the Red Hat identifier in 1998 after reading the poem "Warning" by British writer Jenny Joseph. The poem begins "When I am an old woman I shall wear purple / With a red hat which doesn't go, and doesn't suit me."

Sue Ellen gave a copy of the poem and a red hat to a friend on her fifty-something birthday. Soon there were more friends with more hats, and the group went out to lunch and dubbed themselves the Red Hat Society. A magazine story on the group was picked up by a news wire service and printed on the front page of the *Washington Post*. And word kept spreading.

Red Hats believe in celebrating their age and solidarity and say they meet just to have fun. The fun varies, depending on the chapter. One group's tea party is another's wine tasting. But when they're together they all display the official colors and become a bright sea of red and purple, a color combo that would have given their mothers the vapors. It's not every woman's style, but in 2005 there were more than 850,000 Red Hat members around the world.

Founder Sue Ellen, who goes by the title of Queen Founding Mother and wears large jeweled earrings and a feather boa, credits the Internet for spreading her message so widely and quickly. Reporters often ask Sue Ellen, "But what does this group do?" She answers, "Nothing."

Girls' Night Out Is Good for Your Health

Every so often women get the urge to get together and howl. It keeps us sane. We meet in packs to canoe the lake, camp at the river, and skinny-dip at sunset. We gather in tents, at time-share condos, and on backyard lawns to confide and confess, maybe imbibe too much, laugh too loud, and talk about those things that husbands and partners don't see as important. When winter days grow short, one woman calls another, and she calls one more, and pretty soon they're all playing hooky on a Monday afternoon and sharing soup and bread, a bottle of wine.

Girlfriends fall into a deeper category than social friends or colleagues, although they can evolve from either. Something lets you know you can trust each other, and the friendship grows.

When you get sick or ditched or your child ends up in trouble, your girlfriend is the one who stops by to sit on the bed, tries to fix things, and breaks the gloom with a wisecrack or some sisterly advice, like "Give that sweater to Goodwill."

And as if we didn't already know this, we now have scientific proof that we wouldn't do as well without our pals. UCLA did a study on friendship among women in which researchers made a scientific connection between hanging out with friends and reducing stress. The study indicated that women under stress naturally reach out. This is different from how men react under stress, and like many behavior patterns, the genders' different responses have something to do with ancient survival styles. When threatened, the male would react with the classic "fight-or-flight" response. The female would gather with the women and the babies to feel safe and calm.

The difference in how men and women respond to stress became part of an official study after research workers started noting how their colleagues dealt with angst. When the women in the lab were stressed out they'd make coffee and begin talking about how they felt. The men would go off on their own and hide out. Two women scientists observed this and said, "Aha!" They set about studying this difference, and they even identified the responsible hormone— oxytocin—which encourages a woman's "tend and befriend" response. The researchers said this is another reason women outlive men: social ties, which are more common among women than men, also reduce health risks, by lowering blood pressure, heart rate, and cholesterol.

The Nurses' Health Study from Harvard Medical School provides even more evidence that friendships keep us healthy. The more friends we have, the less likely we are to develop physical problems, said researchers, who claim that not having good buddies is as much of a health risk as being overweight or smoking. For women who lose a spouse, having a close confidante makes the difference between spiraling downward and having the support to get past the black hole days.

Gloria Tells All

The story is now a legend. When Gloria Steinem announced she was forty, a reporter said she didn't look forty, to which Gloria replied, "This is what forty looks like. We've been lying for so long, how would anyone know?"

Obviously, she could have gotten away with being thirty-something for a while longer, and who would have faulted her? Back then, women didn't tell their age freely. The common answer was a "none of your business" grin.

Gloria has admitted that she, too, used to lie about her age, especially to men. But when she turned forty she was a feminist superstar, and a founder of *Ms.* magazine, and she was committed to telling the truth. It was time to bravely tell her age. Through the years Gloria Steinem has shared a lot of personal history—about her abortion, breast cancer, eyelid tuck, becoming a first-time bride at sixty-six. She's spoken, marched, and written on everything from reproductive freedom to changing the electoral college.

Still, even superwomen have age issues. When she turned fifty, she vowed that her strategy would be to act no different than she had in her forties. "Then I realized that doing everything you did before is not progress," she said in a *Mother Jones* interview. Hitting fifty was "like falling off a cliff," she said, because there was no road map for what to do next. Women had followed a certain pattern that dictated how we're supposed to be from adolescence to middle age. After that, there was no plan, or none that Gloria Steinem personally wished to follow. She decided that fifty was another country, and by sixty she seemed to be happily exploring that foreign land.

It felt, she wrote, "like a ten-year-old climbing trees and saying you're not the boss of me, going back to being your obstreperous true self . . . but with your own apartment."

Then came the next decade. "I woke up and there was a seventy-year-old woman in my bed." When she said that to an audience in San Francisco there were gasps and groans all around, because she still doesn't look seventy. The thirty-something sitting next to me said, "No way." For the record, Ms. Steinem was stunning in a squash-colored leather jacket only slightly tawnier than her signature golden hair.

In that San Francisco speech for the Pacific Institute, a think tank that looks at new approaches to aging, Gloria encouraged the mostly middle-aged crowd to speak up and make noise. "This is the beginning of a very major and long overdue movement," she said, fueled by a "great lump of people who are aging" and who are practiced in rebellion. She said we can change the stereotypes, get rid of the "enormous penalty" attached to aging, which particularly hurts women.

As men get older, she said, they fear death and disability. But women, she said, "fear aging itself. We end up fearing those years when we might have the greatest power."

The feminist leader said we need to get together and make aging a positive force. "Sit in small groups and tell the truth to each other and say the unsayable. Be brave and intimate. See age as a gift, not a burden. Then you can stop feeling alone and crazy and paying attention to a culture that says you're wrong."

Tell Your Age, Get Presents

Some consider a birthday party to be a public outing. It's bad enough that the AARP finds out; does the whole world have to, too? Few might have thought to even ask how old you were had it not been for all those stupid black balloons.

But if you can get past that old habit of hiding your age and dreading birthdays, you'll get to relax and enjoy the party. People give you great gifts because by now they know your tastes. One woman I know got lavender from France, soap from Italy, and pot from Oregon for her Sweet Soixante.

TO TELL OR NOT TO TELL?

Why Tell Your Age?

- Gloria will respect you.
- You'll set a good example for your daughters.
- It's on your voter registration records.
- How can you be forty-eight and going to your fortieth high school reunion?

Why Not Tell?

- It's like coming out of any closet. There are minefields out there.
- It's nobody's business.
- Your mother didn't tell hers. Your college roommate's been lying for years.
- You're still getting away with it.

Jan's fiftieth birthday party almost met her wildest fantasy. The party givers were her husband and her best friend, who schemed for months to get it right. They knew what to aim for since Jan, an Indiana attorney, had often said that she wanted to someday have cocktails with Robin Williams, Chris Rock, and other celebs. Her husband actually tried to score a big name, but when that didn't work out Jan's friend found movie posters and created life-size replicas of her fantasy pals.

Arriving for what she'd been told was a small dinner party, Jan walked into her friend's backyard and there were Robin and Chris, Whoopi Goldberg, and NPR's *Car Talk* guys, Click and Clack, standing around the pool. The flesh-and-blood guests were holding up masks of Jan's face.

"I loved it all. I love being the center of attention," Jan says. Friends came from North Carolina and Washington DC to drink martinis with their pal and dine on her favorites, beef tenderloin and garlic mashed potatoes.

Jan might have expected it to be a stellar birthday. Ten years before, on her fortieth birthday, her husband had sent her to Paris for a week of cooking classes at Le Cordon Bleu after conspiring with her secretary to clear her calendar. Maybe it helps to have an inventive husband.

Or to have adoring kids. Holly, from California, spent her sixtieth in Manhattan. A writer and bookstore events planner, Holly celebrated her milestone birthday with friends and family in New York City during one long January weekend. It was her three kids' idea, and her son who lives in Manhattan set everything up.

Holly made up the guest list and twenty-five people attended, the biggest contingent coming from Holly's home state of Ohio, including her former in-laws, who've known Holly since she was fourteen. Two bridesmaids from her 1967 wedding were there. Neither ex-husband came, and no former lovers were invited either.

Everybody stayed at a Washington Square hotel. Holly's room was decorated with banners and flowers. The birthday dinner was at an old Greenwich Village writers' haunt where all the bartenders are off-duty firemen. "There was one big beefy gray-haired guy I would have liked as a birthday present," says Holly.

Over the course of the weekend they went to a swanky bar at Grand Central Station for cocktails, walked in the winter light of Central Park, and had pizza in the Village. For the topper, Holly ice-skated for two hours at Rockefeller Center.

Her kids had also prearranged a surprise family portrait session with a Manhattan fashion photographer. They put Holly in a cab and wouldn't tell her where they were going. "I kept asking, 'Are you taking me to an arranged marriage? Am I getting christened? Did you get me a pony?'" The photographer, she reports, "was British and cute."

You Look Great—
What Have You Done?

S ure, we're vain. How could you be an American woman in the twenty-first century and not have spent a large part of your life considering your looks? You worried over your icky hair when you were a kid, and then your flat chest, and then your wide back and scrawny neck. Was there ever a time when you didn't obsess about some part of your anatomy?

It doesn't stop. You don't wake up at age fifty-three or sixty-two and say, "Where have you been, gorgeous?" It's just that when you get older, you feel a little embarrassed admitting to vanity, as if your great-aunt is watching you preen in the mirror and saying, "Beauty is only skin deep." Maybe we should be above such external concerns, what with all the real disasters going on around us. There you stand, studying your disappearing eyebrows while war, homelessness, and disease should demand your attention.

But why can't those concerns coexist? Surely the finest, most evolved woman has days when she'd give over the grocery money for some miracle cream to wipe away those new lines around her mouth. We humans are externally focused. If someone asks you to describe another person you likely start out with hair color, age, and build before you get to personality traits and intelligence.

We're in good company. The brilliant writer Alice Munro confessed she worried about how her hair looked before she began a book reading. Part of the reason baby boomers spend so much time on their looks is that the media fuels their worries. Vanity concerns sell a lot of moisturizer. Yet, there's evidence that we're not all shallow, self-absorbed mirror-phobes. An AARP survey reported that half of respondents over age fifty accept the changes that come with age and claim to have priorities other than staying and looking young, including family, partner, health and fitness, and a spiritual life.

But the surface issues are there. You can be talking to someone about global warming and still wonder if she bleaches her teeth. Padi, a publicist, was in New York making a pitch to a group of magazine editors. She had only twenty minutes with the last editor, who, Padi was delighted to notice, was staring at Padi with rapt attention. The editor suddenly broke in on Padi's story pitch to ask, "How long have you been letting your gray grow out?"

Padi had always had mounds of red hair, with a personality to match. When her hair started to fade she colored it. But then she took the bold move to let the gray emerge. "I'm from a family of exceedingly vain women, and accepting the changes of age with grace hasn't been graceful. I'm trying. Letting my hair go gray was more for me than the world."

Padi doesn't need a reminder that there are more important priorities. She had breast cancer at the same time her husband was battling prostate cancer. They would make jokes about having so much radiation between them that their bed glowed in the dark. Now in her mid-fifties, Padi says, "I love how I've grown up in the last decade. Knowing myself. Trusting my intuition. Being comfortable in my skin and the world."

And yet, she admits she's not always happy "being middle-aged in a society that values youth and hotness. I don't like how hard this sometimes is for me."

Then there's Leisa, who started working when she was almost thirty, had a baby when she was forty, and has always been at least twelve years older than her closest friends. "Most people don't know how old I am. When I was fifty-two I changed jobs and they took my photo for a press release. I looked at that picture and said, Who is this? It looked like a pre-plastic-surgery photo. I went to my boss and said I needed some time off to get my face done. I did the whole thing. Brows, cheeks, neck. There was no drastic change except it put me back to the age everyone thought I was. My daughter was a little freaked out at first but then she started giving tours so her friends could see me."

"What changed her was what changes all women at fifty. A weight fell away from her; she flew up to a higher perch and cackled a little."
—isak dinesen

TOP FIVE SURGICAL COSMETIC PROCEDURES

1. **Liposuction:** Vacuum device removes fatty tissue from legs, buttocks, abdomen, back, arms, face, and neck.

2. **Breast augmentation:** An implant is inserted behind the muscle between the breast and chest wall.

3. **Eyelid surgery:** Reduces bags beneath the eyes and removes drooping skin on eyelids through an incision in the upper or lower eyelids.

4. **Rhinoplasty:** Alters the size and shape of the bridge and tip of the nose. New scaffolding is made by removing or adding bone and cartilage.

5. **Face-lift:** Various cutting and lifting techniques are used to do exactly what the name implies. Most often an incision is made in the natural contour of the ear, extending around the earlobe and back into the hairline. An incision may also be made under the chin.

Deciding on a New Face

Gini has always enjoyed the notice that comes with being a natural blonde, and hair color is easy enough to hold onto, she says. But in her late fifties, Gini decided her face needed an upgrade. "Being a blonde you draw attention. Someone drives up from behind, sees that you're blonde and pulls alongside. He looks over and smiles. But then he sees your face and speeds ahead."

Experiences like that were just one indication that, as Gini says, "I'd crossed over in terms of my looks. No one was looking anymore." And she didn't like it. Still, it surprised her that she would go as far as a full-on face-lift.

A natural type, Gini doesn't seem like the kind of woman who would consider altering her looks. She wears little makeup, prefers casual clothes, and runs a yoga studio. "I'm probably the total opposite of who you think would do this," she says. "I still feel like this was a slightly shameful thing to do."

She's also been, as she says, "periodically vain." So, out of curiosity she accompanied a friend to an appointment with a well-known San Francisco cosmetic surgeon, and pretty soon the doctor was zeroing in on Gini's face, too. "He took a candid picture of me and put it on a computer screen and then started eradicating this and that. Once you begin to see what you would look like, who can say no?"

A British-born poet, Gini has a nervous elegance, partially due to a Julie Christie–like accent that upgrades anything she says, even when she's reading some of her more randy poems. She has a playful side and a formal side. A big part of her social life involves attending the opera with her husband, and that's where she first started feeling discomfort over her looks. The prescribed uniform of evening gowns with décolleté made her feel exposed, "looking like a full-blown elderly plate of raw meat." It didn't help that other opera regulars of her age group were constantly looking younger. And the more poetry she published, the more readings she was called on to perform, and that also made her self-conscious. "I decided I wanted to take my next bow with a face-lift."

The surgery cost $15,000 and took place over two long sessions. She pulls back her bangs and twists her ears to show the thin white lines from the surgery, as if she were revealing the nicks in a fine piece of furniture. Her doctor, she says, is known as "the best closer in the business." She liked that he was a Vietnam vet, even though, she says, "he probably learned his craft putting back faces blown apart from battle before catering to pampered socialites."

He called her "dear" and said that most of his patients were "women who simply wanted to look their best—strong, proactive women like me. I let him think I was a strong woman and didn't confess to all my periods of self-pity."

TOP FIVE NONSURGICAL COSMETIC PROCEDURES

1. **Botox injection:** Biological toxins are injected into the forehead with tiny needles to numb the muscle so it won't contract. This smoothes frown lines and crow's-feet.

2. **Laser hair removal:** A laser passes through the skin and disables hair follicles.

3. **Chemical peel:** The skin's top layer is peeled off by applying a chemical solution to sun-damaged, uneven-pigmented, or finely wrinkled facial tissue.

4. **Microdermabrasion:** A mild abrasion or polishing process is used to remove dead cells and reduce fine lines, age spots, and acne scars.

5. **Hyaluronic acid:** This acid is injected along the edge of a wrinkle or line to be erased, often used on folds along the nose and sides of the mouth.

Unfortunately, her recovery was "horrific." She camped out at a friend's house for a couple of weeks, loaded on painkillers and dreading what would emerge from the bandages. She scribbled poetry about "my blow-torched face, this bubbling mess." She chastised herself for "cutting off all my charm and God-given real face."

But today Gini sits on a pale green couch in front of her bay view, in full sun, her skin smooth, her eyes bright. She says her surgery didn't turn her into a brand-new person. "You think it will, like when you have a child or get your first poem published." But she's still glad she did it, even though it took several months before she felt comfortable with her new face. "At first you look like a rat in a wind tunnel. One of my friends asked if I'd been in a bicycling accident."

Eventually people started telling her she looked great and asking if she'd been on a long vacation. But her husband disapproved. "He said he didn't see why I had to do this. He said he preferred the way I looked before." Gini laughs wryly at that, because among her many reasons for getting a face-lift was to save her bumpy marriage. "I wanted a few more years of looking good and I wanted to help my marriage. I didn't really acknowledge that was one of my motives until after I had it done."

The marriage is still in limbo, but even if it finally breaks apart Gini says her new face has given her "confidence in myself I never had." She says that she no longer feels anonymous, that people take her for fifteen years younger than she is, and that it makes her feel "back on the map sexually."

Future Freak-Out

My personal concern about plastic surgery is that we'll go too far. I have daughters in their thirties and was with one of them at a women's event in San Francisco. Most of the people in the crowd were of middle age or older, and I asked her whether she could see any face-lifts in the crowd.

"Not one, and that's good," she said. "Because when you're older and trying to look younger, you actually look older. And if you're trying too hard to not look your age, that reinforces the idea that older is bad and younger girls are way hotter."

I will add that this thirty-something woman has wondered what will happen by the time she's fifty. Or forty. Will a surgical makeover be as common as a bikini waxing? Will women feel compelled to get the alteration du jour?

In 2004 a Chinese beauty pageant was held in which all the contestants had had plastic surgery. That was the idea—to see who had the best surgical remodeling. One of the contestants rationalized, "Isn't everyone artificial in some way?"

She had a point. We shave the God-given hair off our legs, boost our cleavage, color our hair. We want the straightest, whitest teeth that money, or health insurance, can buy. What if we started going in just as routinely to have our faces overhauled?

Most aging boomers have decided to live with their looks, for political and practical reasons. Only 25 percent of cosmetic surgeries in 2004 were performed on people between fifty-one and sixty-four. It doesn't yet feel like a job requirement. Cosmetic surgery is still risky and costly. There are no guarantees that it will change your life and buy you love. Besides, your health plan probably doesn't cover it. If you're worried about the lines on your forehead, you can grow bangs.

But what if the procedures that are iffy today become affordable, safe, and as common as adult orthodontia? Talk about peer pressure. What if everyone at your high school reunion or in your book club started going for it? Our generation has the option of being made over. But will our daughters have a choice? What if they all end up looking the same, with those big eyes, that tiny nose, and a profile made out of steel, looking not a day over twenty-nine?

Who Are We Trying
to Kid?

This cosmetic surgery question is a pesky one. You can be philosophically opposed to the whole thing because there are so many more important qualities than an unlined face. But then there are those days. "I look in the mirror and say, 'You look like shit,'" says Celeste, who wishes her face were as toned and youthful looking as the rest of her fifty-two-year-old body. "Why can't we work on our faces at the gym?" she moans, running her fingers through freshly colored golden curls and sipping a nonfat latte.

Celeste, a photographer, admits that she feels "horrible pressure" to do like most of her middle-aged girlfriends and get some work done—tattooed eyeliner, collagen plumping, lid lifts, or even a full-on face-lift. She says she's practically the only woman in her crowd who hasn't had a makeover.

"I was surprised at first that I would know even one woman who'd have cosmetic surgery, but then I heard about a friend. Then another. I saw a woman I knew at a party and I could tell she'd done something because she looked awesome. Another had the works. She showed up at a meeting and a man I know kept staring at her. He said, 'Boy, I hope my wife gets that done when she's that age.' I sat there feeling like dumpy-the-lumpy.

"I'm not a beautiful woman and I've always felt like my greatest attraction was my personality. Off and on for the past five years I've thought a lot about cosmetic surgery, but then I saw a show on TV where the doctor was peeling back the flesh and then stapling things into a woman's head. What if I had my eyes done and they did one wrong? If I go to the beauty shop and my hair color is a shade wrong or cut one inch too short I freak out. You hear about people getting their eyes done and then one doesn't shut right."

She did go as far as Botox. "I have deep creases between my eyes, which probably come from being an artist. I thought Botox would be a good segue into the next step. I spent $300 and it lasted three weeks. The creases were smoothed out. My forehead didn't move. But for a week and a half I had a horrible headache."

For the present Celeste says she'll try to maintain her personal flash through her signature look—tight blue jeans, silver belt, and Tiffany necklace. And she'll continue to chide herself. "Sometimes I think the only one who's worrying about how I look is me. After all, who am I trying to fake out? The busboy?"

The Next You

In her fifties Chris began teaching skiing to disabled people on Vancouver Island. This was after running a sheep farm, working as a nurse's aide and hospice worker, raising two kids, growing prize dahlias, marrying, divorcing, and living with a man who committed suicide. No wonder she likes her white, quiet world.

"I adore skiing, and giving others the marvelous opportunity of gliding on velvet is a gift," says Chris. Her clients are blind, autistic, or paraplegic; some have Down's

REASONS TO DO IT

1. Your friends are doing it and you're tired of being asked if you're their auntie.

2. You want it, you can afford it, and you trust your doctor.

3. Your son's getting married and you want to look better in the wedding photos than the mother of the bride.

4. It will make you happy.

REASONS TO PASS

1. Who wants to be another sap for the beauty culture? Give the money to the food bank or go back to law school.

2. You can let your hair blow in the wind and not worry about showing those telltale white scars along your hairline.

3. People die, like Olivia Goldsmith (author of *The First Wives Club*), dead at age fifty-four following complications during cosmetic surgery.

4. The effects of cosmetic procedures don't all last. You may have to do it again. And again.

syndrome. "I feel like I'm their way to freedom and fun," says Chris. "They feel so proud to discover they have this sport in their veins."

Chris lived most of her life in New England. Now Canada feels like home. Being a midlife woman in Canada she says is "absolutely wonderful," since it offers affordable medical care, free ferries, good second-hand stores, and no pressure to color your hair. "Few women on my island dye their gray."

Chris lives on a small pension, and her small house, with a forest in the backyard and a view of a summer stream from her kitchen window, is paid for. When she moved to Vancouver Island she made friends by joining two kayaking clubs, a hiking club, and an exercise group. Although she lives alone, she has boyfriends and a daughter who lives nearby. "I have happy and nurturing people all around me. A lot of people live with less here than they could other places. But somehow all this nature helps people love themselves." Her mentor skied until the age of eighty-three, and Chris's current role model and hiking buddy is "a radical and a beauty in her eighties whose mission is saving bears."

Kate, who is single and works in wine marketing, gave herself English riding lessons, both to prepare for a dream vacation of riding horses in Ireland and to relive the thrill of "feeling as free as a twelve-year-old." She still takes a private riding class one hour a week and says one of the best things about riding is how it focuses her mind on the moment.

"You can't be thinking about anything else but you and the horse. The slightest movement from your body is a signal for the horse to do something, so you have to be very aware. Someone warned me that horseback riding is one of the most dangerous sports there is, but it makes me feel alive. When I started lessons I asked the instructor if I was too old to ride. She said she has seventy-year-olds coming in for their first lesson."

Then there's Hillary, a businesswoman and longtime opera fan who began taking classical voice lessons in her fifties. Not to please an audience but to please herself. "I've sung all my life, sometimes in choirs but mostly for myself. As a teen I would come home after school and sit at the piano or play the guitar and wail my heart out." When she had kids she made sure they had dance, music, and voice lessons, "the things I wanted to do myself." When she was in her forties she joined a community theater group and sang in the chorus, alongside mostly sixteen- to twenty-year-olds.

She takes a voice lesson once a week. "I think of it as my therapy, meditation, and yoga. The deep breathing, placement, and focus are energizing, relaxing, and often exhilarating. I also sometimes hear the voice that I would like to have. Singing fills me up. It even makes me feel taller."

Often on a summer evening the residents of Babs's condo building will ask her to keep her doors and windows open to hear her play the piano. "It makes me feel like I've unleashed a dormant musician inside of me," she says. A geographer and cartographer for a California city, Babs started taking piano lessons when she was fifty-three. She had stopped teaching an evening class in software and decided to use that time doing "something creative." She found a used piano in the classified ads and that New Year's Eve pledged to make her new year "one of joy-filled creative expression."

Babs grew up with a piano in the house, and when she was a young girl she taught herself to play, "but just with the right hand, using a beginner's piano book and a hymnal. My mom taught me how to chord but I always longed to take real lessons and play with both hands. We couldn't afford lessons, and when I became a single mom on a budget I couldn't indulge myself. Finally I became financially stable and had time to get busy and learn something new."

For her the thrill of playing is "hitting the right notes, the wonderful sound of dissonant chords coming back to resonance. Playing brings me back to the present. I forget my day or what else I have to do. Playing takes me to a grand ballroom or a concert hall. Sometimes I picture people dancing to my playing." The piano has also introduced her to other late-blooming musicians. "We play together, give each other tips."

Fabric artist Virginia Harris took an early out from corporate life in New York and at fifty-five moved to California to teach herself how to quilt. She uses the old, homey art as a political statement. Virginia's highly sought after quilts, which hang in the Smithsonian and other museums, contain Virginia's edgy opinions on racism, imperialism, world conflict, and whatever she reads in the news that makes her blood boil. She's created a 9/11 quilt and a KKK quilt. She chose the artist's life after going through what she calls "my American Dream phase—the house, the cars, the husband, the three vacations a year. I took an early retirement and said, I'm through. I want to quilt."

After years of working as an AIDS nurse, Marsha lost her job when her hospital position was eliminated. Depressed at being booted from a job that was so much of her identity, but with a good-sized severance package in hand, she became a ski bum for the winter, working at a Lake Tahoe resort in the race department for $7.50 an hour. "I loved every minute. Depressed? Hahahahaha."

Desert Changes

Santa Fe is an encouraging place to be middle aged, says Billie Blair, president of her community foundation. "Your face doesn't have to be tucked and you don't have to have a man by your side. People our age keep reinventing themselves, hoping they'll get it right. Santa Fesinas don't worry about being middle aged. Mostly we're boomers, many are survivors of the hippie years and think we're forever young. We don't intend to die with the music still in us."

A newspaper publisher before she began heading the foundation, Billie says what she likes about her new job is that she gets to "carry water in this high desert for good, caring, interesting people who want to make this a better community. I like interacting with human beings, which is why I'm in this profession."

Her fifties have been a time for exploring. "I did the requisite year in Europe in my twenties, but my fifties have taken me to hike the Inca Trail to Machu Picchu in Peru, to Cuba, to Vietnam and Libya. I can still travel on the cheap but now I require a toilet seat and no cockroaches." She regularly takes off for a mountain cabin with no running water, "a place my husband and I got before all the breathing air was gone." And she's devoted to her Pilates class, "where I would go even if it meant taking money from the hairdresser and letting my hair go gray."

For her next career, Billie says, "I know that when I'm ready to close this door another will be open." Hopefully, she says, it will be something "where I'm only responsible for my own work—maybe writing, teaching abroad, being a full-time volunteer. I cannot fathom not working at something that helps heal the world."

New Act for the Mommies

In the 1990s, two housewives in Petaluma, California, decided they had some funny things to share about being mothers. Calling themselves "The Mommies," they put together a comedy routine that became popular at women's gatherings in their hometown. Word spread, and they got some out-of-town bookings, sometimes adding another comic to the show, sometimes throwing in music and funny costumes. But it was basically Marilyn Kentz, the one with the brown hair, and Caryl Kristensen, the blonde, yakking about husbands and teenage kids and suburban paralysis.

The show went big time and became a TV sitcom, then a comedy special and a TV talk show featuring Caryl and Marilyn. Eventually it came time for the two to peaceably go their separate ways. Marilyn changed her focus from motherhood to middle age and wrote a book, *Fearless Women: Midlife Portraits,* and developed a performance piece called *Boomer Babes.* Caryl went back to school and became a college adviser for high school kids.

The two Mommies stayed in Los Angeles after their TV shows ended. Marilyn concedes that it's a challenging place to live middle age in a brazen, open way. "Everyone's a swan in LA. But that helped position my attitude. I wasn't going to go down with a whimper, thinking I'm not good enough because all these young women with taut skin and puffed-up lips are better than me. Maybe it's the Prozac, but I can turn it around and appreciate the young women's naïveté and their need for approval. At their young age I thought I had it all and what society said I needed. When we're young we have our most appealing bodies and when we're older we have wisdom and strength. I think it's part of the plan, either from God or nature, that you have to be attractive so you can procreate and the human race continues. If we were strong and wise and not so approval needy when we were young we'd be saying to the men, 'Get out of here.'"

It's one thing to make fun of being an exhausted housewife and mother, which Marilyn did in "The Mommies." It's another to be out there as a middle-aged woman in *Boomer Babes,* talking about her empty nest, her own ailing mother, and a belly that refuses to become flat. But she finds that women are ready to laugh and cry together about the good and bad stuff of aging.

"There are millions of boomers trying to find where we belong. Boomers won't go out without a fight. We need to teach women you don't have to feel bad about getting older. If it's all about being sexy and looking sexy, we'll lose. We can't compete with younger women on that and we shouldn't try to."

Still, she says, "In LA it's hard not to get compared. You just have to find a strong posse of strong women to make you feel better. The way to fear less about aging is to get your support system intact. I do a monologue on our parents' decline and death. That's when you need to know you're not alone."

Marilyn has come to appreciate the confidence of certain older women. "Women who exude a passion for life from deep within can be the most alluring women in the room no matter where their breasts land. The exterior then gets its own little glow from that confidence."

The other ex-Mommie, Caryl, says she's on her third career and jokes, "I'm afraid of face-lifts so I had to get out of television." She still dabbles in TV work and does public speaking through her business, a service that walks high school students and their parents through the college application experience.

"I loved the process of finding colleges for my kids. The searching, visiting, touring. And then I started helping other kids. Finally someone told me I was good at this and should open up a business." So she went back to college, got a certificate in college counseling, and opened up her practice with a professor who helps kids prepare for undergraduate admission tests.

About her TV years, Caryl says, "It was a big adventure. I still have friends in the business. We still get invited to premieres. The excitement of the business is undeniable. But when 'The Mommies' dried up, it was time to move on. I didn't have anything left to say. Or maybe I didn't have a need to purge on stage. I also got tired of waiting for someone else to tell me I'm good enough to work. So I went off and started something else."

"You don't get to choose how you're going to die or when. You can only really decide how you're going to live." —joan baez

Following Sandra Wallace's strategy, think about what's next for you. Considering the questions below may help you figure it out.

- What do you always say you wish you had more time for?

- What do you dabble in now and dream of going whole hog over?

- What did you once love doing before you became a career woman, wife, mother, grandmother, caregiver to the universe?

- What makes you smile when you're doing it?

- What would you do if you didn't worry that someone would say, "You're kidding. At your age?"

- What was the last risk you took?

- In five years, when someone asks what you do, what do you want to be able to say?

Plan the Dream

Hang gliding. Studying Russian history. Opening a bookstore. Sitting in the hammock and staring at the clouds. After fifty, the attitude should be "It's my turn now, dammit," and even if it's still a few credit card payments off, you can start thinking about what your dream might be. You can even plan for it.

Three women counselors in Seattle, recognizing that wishful thinking may be part of good planning, developed a brainstorming program for women called New Choices. It's a six-week program that helps women figure out how to plan for the next part of life. The idea, they say, is to encourage women to take advantage of the next thirty years or so instead of sleepwalking into the sunset.

It's not therapy or a workshop. Nobody gives lectures. There's a facilitator and a group of ten women. Some nights they talk about money; other nights the subject is how to know when you're having fun. They're all roughly middle aged, and many don't know each other, but they're all trying to figure out their passions. No one comes out of the six weeks with a business plan to open a bead factory in Peru, but together they spark some great notions.

It's that kind of open-ended, blue-sky thinking that makes the Seattle program so popular. Within six months of starting out, they had a long waiting list, says New Choices founder Sandra Wallace, who at seventy continues to work part-time at her counseling job while helping to run New Choices.

"The second half of your life is not as ego driven," says Sandra. "It's more about satisfaction. Some people like me are going to work until they're seventy. Some are financially set and retire but then they get bored. Even travel, if it's the only thing, gets old." Sandra was surprised at how many women admitted "they hadn't really thought about what they'd do with the rest of their lives or just assumed it would all work out.

"I know a fifty-eight-year-old woman working at a high-tech company and putting in eighty hours a week. She's not unusual. A lot of working women feel they have no time left over to do what they want. I call them overfunctioning. Maybe they need to reframe their job. We're such a driven country, you feel you have to account for yourself all the time. People put down older people if they're not working, volunteering, or doing something," says Sandra. "Whatever gives you satisfaction, that's important," says Sandra. "Who cares, even if it's golf?"

Still Looking for Your Red Shoes?

On the other side of the country, in Baton Rouge, Louisiana, Roberta Guillory used her inheritance money to launch a women's program called The Red Shoes, "a place dedicated to women's inner life and creativity." Many clients are businesswomen, "the type who find it easier to work on their inner lives if they make an appointment." They do their spiritual work through dance, book studies, discussion groups, and retreats.

Her program is named after the Hans Christian Andersen story but inspired by Jungian analyst and writer Clarissa Pinkola Estés's interpretation of the tale. In *Women Who Run with the*

Wolves, Estés wrote of the importance for each woman to find the shoes that uniquely fit her feet, instead of forcing herself into ill-fitting shoes just to please someone else.

The aim of Roberta's The Red Shoes is to "celebrate, support, and empower women" through classes that range from tango to intuitive painting. It also offers a spiritual smorgasbord— Passover gatherings, lectures in Islam, Christian prayer groups. "I wanted it ecumenical because in our society so many people stay in their own little corners." The Red Shoes also provides practical assistance, offering rentable office space to professional women who need a place to conduct business outside their home a few hours a week.

"It's usually the women in middle age who are asking the question 'Who am I and what do I want for myself now that my children are grown?'" says Roberta. "I'm amazed how many women come in and are frank enough to say they don't know who they are. Or what they really want, even though they are very dedicated to pleasing their husbands, mothers, and children and doing really good things for their community. Southern women have had a great influence behind the scenes, but it has not been their style to openly speak their truth, especially if it conflicts with the male point of view."

Roberta has a master's degree in social work, but she's devoted her primary life work to spiritual training, which has included spending time at a New Mexico monastery and studying with Jungian analyst and author Jean Shinoda Bolen *(Goddesses in Everywoman* and *The Millionth Circle).* "I've always seen the unity in the psychological and the spiritual."

Roberta's message about feminine energy being necessary to save the planet doesn't always go over in her conservative part of the country, but she insists, "At this time in history we need the balance of the feminine and the masculine to have a healthy society. We've never lived in a society where there is a balance. It's always been a patriarchy where we have wars, dissension, and violence. Women have always been the peacemakers who held the home and hearth together. It's time for that feminine energy to be put out there."

After a marriage of some forty years, Roberta now lives alone in her pink Victorian house on a lake in Baton Rouge. She and her former husband are friends, but she says, "I'm a contemplative mystical person by nature. I love people, but at this stage of life I have to have my silence."

The Importance of Being Techy

Leisa Holland-Nelson in Houston didn't set out to be a high-tech queen. She used to work in the New York fashion world, first as a buyer and then as a vice president for a fashion house. But she says that the computer world is as smart and innovative, and maybe even as sexy, as the latest hot styles used to be. "Fashion was an important trendy business twenty years ago. And that's what the Internet and technology are now. Techno geeks and venture capitalists in Houston are like rock stars."

Leisa runs an Internet company in Houston and admits that she's not that much of a techno whiz. "My partners are the engineers and I have friends who are miles ahead of me on technology. But what I do understand is what people need and how to get it."

Any woman who wants to stay a player in the modern world, says Leisa, needs to know how to get it, too. "Being unfamiliar with technology is not an option. If you want to be in touch with business or just your children, you need e-mail, text messaging, and whatever comes up next. You want to know what's next. It's all about being in touch. The Internet has opened up the whole world and I can't imagine choosing not to be part of it.

"I personally don't know how to build a Web site but I can get involved with someone's site and make it great. Everyone goes to a Web site to get information. The Internet is so important. You can even Google someone who's asked you for a date. Stuff shows up. If you want to know

WHY, AT MY AGE, SHOULD I GO HIGH TECH?

- It really started out as a women-dominated field. Women were the first computer programmers.
- These are not electronic tools; they're necessities.
- Technology helps you better navigate your life.
- It keeps you in touch with everyone in your life (sisters, ex-lovers, and so on) anywhere in the world.
- You'll need it for your next job.
- Today's cutting edge will become common.
- You can search for your old high school sweetheart online, or for the best deal on Egyptian cotton sheets.
- Learn almost as much about those funny skin tags as you would from your doctor.
- You can fight the stereotype: getting older doesn't mean that you have to be annoyed by new gadgets.

about a business you go to their site. You might be able to find articles in the newspaper about a major business, but for the smaller ones you need to go to their Web site."

Leisa fell into the world of the Web after making a huge career and lifestyle change in her early fifties. She had had a long-term marriage, become a first-time mother at age forty, and held a position as executive vice president for a fashion house.

"I felt totally fulfilled and never expected my life to change. Then I got fired." So Leisa and her family moved to New Jersey, where she tried a couple of other jobs before taking a position with an executive search company.

Then her marriage of twenty-one years ended. She became a single parent, was lured by her mother and stepfather back to Houston, her hometown, and began looking for a way to pay the bills.

"Everything in my life changed when I got a divorce. We came to Houston really with nothing, even though my ex-husband and I had sold a big house and split the money. I was so busy getting out of New Jersey and moving I didn't realize I was wounded until two years later. I had never taken a breath, never grieved the end of my twenty-one year marriage."

Her stepfather gave her financial backing to launch her second entrepreneurial venture, her Internet business, and now she's starting to enjoy this new life. "There's a part of starting over that is energizing. I love the idea of growing a business and changing it, even though I'm not as financially secure as I'd like to be.

"But I've become incredibly involved in the city and am meeting the people who are making big changes here. Because I live here it's important to be involved in the community and the issues, for my daughter's sake and for my business's sake. There wasn't a lot of money to market the business and I had to get out and network. I met a top public relations person for the technology industry in Houston, who was a critical part of my business development. She taught me how to network in Houston. She said you can be going to one hundred events a week, but you can't be an effective networker if you're exhausted. Now, I call her and ask if I should go to something."

To keep up her energy Leisa adheres to a strict exercise schedule. "I really need to feel good and in order to do that I have to be in good shape. Yoga, kickboxing, spinning, running, going for a big walk. I need to exercise. It's the only thing in my life that is all mine. I don't know if I'll ever get to rock on the front porch. I'm not a good sit-around person. I've been lucky that I've never needed to slow down. Except now, some mornings I roll over and stay in bed until 6:30."

HOW TO GET HIP ON HIGH TECH

- Take a computer class at a community college, where there's no such thing as a stupid question.

- Have a teenager on call to troubleshoot. Borrow the next-door neighbor's if you don't have your own in-house computer geek.

- Read the Circuits section of the *New York Times*.

- Go on the Internet and find out the basics of some new gadget, study the info, come up with your questions, and walk away from any salesperson who doesn't kindly, thoroughly, and respectfully answer each one. Or who tells you to have your husband teach you.

- Expect that some new gizmos are going to take more time and patience to master than others.

- Never throw away the manual.

Keep On Keeping On

There are a few of us who are doing a version of the same job or career we started with. Sometimes you may wonder if you're easily satisfied or unimaginative, especially when an old acquaintance you haven't seen since your hair was in a flip resurfaces and asks, "Are you *still* doing that?"

It's possible that some of us just chose the right major in college or lucked out and found our life's work early, even though the common notion today is that most people will have four or five different jobs in a lifetime.

As a journalist I like to think about reporter Helen Thomas, who has aggressively covered the White House for more than sixty years. When she received a journalism award at age eighty-one, she complained that people always comment on her age. "I get this all the time: How can she still be working? Why isn't she retired? Why doesn't she drop dead?" Reporting is her job and what she loves to do, she said, and her goal is always to be a better reporter. "It's a constant learning game, and I'm still learning."

Then there's Jane Scott, a *Cleveland Plain Dealer* reporter who worked as a rock critic until she was eighty-two. She was known for her blonde hair and red glasses and a fascination with an art form that is thought of as belonging to and defined by youth. She once said, "If you know what you're doing you don't have to think about your age."

And if you feel like you're always learning something new, then you get to keep reinventing the job along with yourself.

One of the beauties of being a teacher is that "you spend your whole life being around people who are trying to be the best they can be," says Eve, a sociology professor in Boston. "Teaching is a gift," she says. "You're with people who are on an exciting journey. Every class is new."

Because so many faculty members are over age fifty-five and there's no mandatory retirement age, Eve's university and others influence seasoned professors to stay challenged and excited about their work. "They do things to support our creativity. Encourage people to go to professional conferences and workshops, to meet with colleagues from different universities. This way you keep developing yourself.

"My baseline is I love what I do. I gravitated toward my profession because of family dynamics. My father would have been an academic but in the Holocaust he got displaced and ended up an office worker. My job was to put the family back on track. I grew up where the academic world was talked about as the lost Eden."

When Eve was a freshman in college she had a role model who was an anthropology professor. "I remember her talking about what all mammals have in common, and it was like she was bringing order out of chaos. She was so wise and what I wanted to be when I grew up."

Eve mentors her students more than she does junior faculty. "I have an ongoing relationship with some of my students. We wind up having off-line conversations about life. To be around bright people is delicious. It keeps you young. I'm never involved in conversations about physical illness and decline."

Arlone is a hospital administrator and nurse recruiter and consumate Patriots fan who lives in the north shore area of Boston. Arlone has been involved in some form of nursing her entire adult life, like her mother before her, who worked as a registered nurse at a veterans' hospital in Buffalo, New York, until she was seventy-nine. Now in her mid-fifties, Arlone doesn't see any reason she won't work as long.

"If you're doing direct-care nursing the job can be harsh. Taking care of patients, bending, stooping, pushing, pulling, and the mental pressure does wear on you and your health. But now in nursing management I don't feel the same wear and tear. Primarily I'm exercising my brain. I see myself working for a very long time. It's who I am. Unless I become ill or injured, I can still use my mind and practice as long as I want. Nursing is something that becomes meshed with your identity."

Working in an acute-care hospital north of Boston and also as a recruiter for a nursing service, Arlone says nursing keeps her intellectually challenged. "It sounds a little too altruistic to just say I want to help people. There is that, but I like using my brain, acquiring knowledge, and then seeing good outcomes. Medical people are always going back to class, always getting certification and learning. I've been in and out of grad schools three times and I'm not done yet. Right now I'm not at the top of my field but that could still happen. I've been told I'd make a great educator. That may be next."

She admits she's not wild about being in her fifties. "I preferred my thirties. I hit my stride then. I was taken seriously, on my way in my career. I was starting to feel successful. I crewed on a sailboat. I really liked myself at thirty. Sometimes when I'm talking about life experiences someone will ask, 'How old are you, anyway?' I ask them how old they think. They usually guess ten years younger."

Although she was married once for five years, Arlone has been single now for more than twenty. "I haven't done a lot of dating since I was in my forties. If I did date it would be someone younger, but that probably won't happen because I'm not Demi Moore. I'd like someone who has his own money, a brain, not quite the boy toy, but appealing to the eye." She's not interested in men her own age because, she says, they're too frail or needy. "They've got one foot in the grave and the other on a banana peel."

Working in public relations allowed Flo to work out of her home long before telecommuting became a common option. But you have to push to stay current in the field, says Flo, a public relations consultant in Los Angeles. "Between the isolation and the cats sitting on top of my computer and my newspapers, it sometimes feels like a prison. I crave any opportunity to get out and interact with live people."

Mixing it up with other professionals is one thing that keeps her going. About attending a breakfast meeting with other PR types, she says, "Every time I go to one of these I come out re-energized. I love the opportunity to learn and the exchange of ideas."

An advantage of working from home, says Flo, is that "people don't know how old I am since I don't sound old and I can talk to anyone on their level. It's a skill I learned long ago and which I'm good at. One PR guy I know is eighty-seven and he's still working full-time. I've rarely found age to be a factor in public relations. More important is being youthful in attitude and demeanor and being able to keep up with skills. What holds people back is that attitude about 'you can't teach an old dog new tricks.' If someone says they can't get the hang of some technology, that person will be left behind."

Always Camera Ready

I f you're going to stay at the top, you have to be flexible and keep an eye out for sharks. TV anchorwoman Barbara Rodgers knows about doing both. Barbara's in a business that skews toward younger people. "Look at the anchor teams at most places. The guy is older, sometimes plump, sometimes balding, often gray, and the woman looks youthful and doesn't have gray hair."

Barbara, a longtime San Francisco Bay Area TV personality, is one of the exceptions. "I look at the women past fifty in my business. Diane Sawyer, Leslie Stahl. We all still look pretty good. Barbara Walters is seventy-something. That gives me lots of latitude."

Still, Barbara had to fight to keep her place, in a struggle that became a lively public debate. It started about the time she decided to stop dying her hair. "When I was about forty-seven I thought for me to act like I didn't have any gray hair wasn't realistic. So I let it go natural.

TUBE TOMATOES & OTHER MEDIA

Think of the visible, dynamic, ground-breaking, mature media women who don't stoop to what Ellen Goodman calls "food fight journalism" but report in tough, savvy, and often delightful ways.

Some favorites. You add yours.

TV:

- Linda Ellerbee
- Elizabeth Farnsworth
- Gwen Ifill
- Meredith Viera
- Oprah Winfrey

Print:

- Maureen Dowd
- Ellen Goodman
- Arianna Huffington
- Molly Ivins
- Anna Quindlen

Radio:

- Anne Garrels
- Terry Gross
- Cokie Roberts
- Susan Stamberg
- Nina Totenberg

I got such positive responses from viewers. It became my trademark, this gray streak."

Her bosses' opinions were another matter. "They said the gray was nice, but they ended up firing me." Her termination at the CBS affiliate became a big public issue. Why they let her go was never defined, but since she was a woman, over age forty, and African-American, her supporters cried racism, sexism, and ageism.

"There was a huge public response. I think the station was somewhat shocked by it." Barbara got an attorney, sued for breach of contract, and won her job back, and now those bosses are long gone. Barbara has gone on to scoop up national and regional awards, including a number of Emmys for reporting and anchoring. In 2004 the National Association of Black Journalists declared October 15 to be Barbara Rodgers Day, on the anniversary of her twenty-fifth year with CBS 5 Eyewitness News (KPIX-TV). The League of Women Voters gave her a "Woman Who Could Be President" award.

She continues to push herself, she says, because of the changing nature of the TV business and the need for all TV people, particularly veterans, to stay flexible. "Those who don't transition well after forty are the ones not open to change. You're always going to have managers who don't see things the same as you, like the ones who fired me. I never knew what their reasons were. Maybe they wanted to change the team, to replace me with a much younger person. I have always been willing to make changes. Take on new assignments. Do different shows. Work weekends, special assignments.

"People don't want us if we dig our heels in. If you embrace change and make it work for you and not against you, it gives you much more marketability. You need to keep learning. Learn the new equipment and adjust to it. I remember when we went from manual typewriters to computers. Some of the older people were freaked out. That dooms you when you say, 'I hate this,' because they're not going to say, 'Okay then, we'll let you keep the typewriter.' Of course, the computer was so much better. It enhanced my writing."

For the most part, Barbara has loved her fifties. "I tell young women in their twenties and thirties that fifty is the best-kept secret," says Barbara. "I didn't know it was going to be so much fun in my fifties. I'm not sure but I think there is a kind of freedom that comes with fifty—a freedom and a focus.

"When men turn fifty I think they panic and believe they're getting old. Women used to, but now we see it opening a door of possibilities. I'm not sure what changed, but I think it was us. Women changed their minds about what old is. We did it collectively. We saw women not being kicked out the door but starting something new in their profession. Doing all this stuff and also looking beautiful."

When Barbara hit fifty she made two major changes in her life—she hired a personal trainer and she got a divorce. "I had a real surge of energy. Things I wanted to do. My fiftieth birthday present to myself was a trainer. It's not so much about vanity as feeling good. I know enough about the medical aspects of strength training that it might prevent osteoporosis and keep my muscles in shape. I want my body to be healthy. I'm stronger now than I was in my thirties because I lift weights. I look better than I did in my thirties. I eat better than I did in my thirties. I am better than I was in my thirties."

Her divorce came when she was fifty-two, after twenty-five years of marriage. When she started dating again, she found that "it's great fun. Dating is very different than in my twenties. There are plenty of interesting and fun men to date." Including, she says, a number of younger men.

"Two weeks after I split up I started getting asked out by younger men who said they'd been eying me for a while. I asked them why were they so determined to go out with me. They said I was more interesting than the younger women. The younger women wanted to talk about clothes, getting married, and having babies." It was another part of the post-fifty learning experience—"to find out that knowledge and experience are attractive qualities."

At age fifty-eight, Barbara, who has a house in the suburbs, gave herself another birthday present—a weekend studio apartment in San Francisco.

"My sister died suddenly at age sixty-one. I'd never thought of her not being around to grow old with me. She always talked about the things she'd do some day. Another friend of mine got hit by a truck. I've always said you should embrace life and that we are never promised anything more than this moment."

So, now she has her pied-à-terre. "My friends come over and we drink champagne on the balcony and look at the view. Maybe it's money I'll need in retirement, but I'll worry about that when I get there."

"If you obey all the rules you miss all the fun."
—katharine hepburn

Change for the Future

The stereotype has it that the older you get, the less flexible you are. People become stodgy, closed down, predictable, rigid, stuck in the old ways. They're averse to new products, strange ideas, exotic foods, bizarre music. But another word for change is regeneration. Change, good or bad, is about the future.

By this age we're pretty practiced at adapting to life's altering forces. There are changes that we have no choice but to accept. A layoff notice, kids in trouble, divorce, a death in the family—these are the unwelcome changes we know to be part of life.

But good change is also a part of living—a challenging computer program that lets you know your mind is still working, a new author who makes you think, a sudden impulse that causes you to take down the living room wall so you can have house concerts. There are so many delightful ways to do the unexpected.

Like TV anchor Barbara Rodgers says, things change and you need to adapt if you want to remain a player. Change can be a reminder to keep moving forward. Besides, the more we embrace change, the more we change the stereotype that we refuse to.

Do the Thing You Wouldn't Dare

My colleague Mary Fricker, widowed twice, is a tireless investigative reporter who cares about immigrants, workers' rights, and justice for all. She coauthored an exposé on the savings and loans industry called "Inside Job: The Looting of America's Savings and Loans." Ever the adventurer, she spent one summer vacation on a cattle drive and herded cows from Susanville, California, to the winter range in Nevada. But in her soul, Mary's a surfer.

SCARY IS GOOD

Flying through the air on a trapeze isn't for everyone. For some of us it's daring enough to drive into a strange town without a hotel reservation. There are many ways to push yourself into that uncertain place where accomplishment feels so good. Just make sure you wear a helmet and take care of your bones. Then do what scares you but won't actually kill you, such as the following:

- Ask a friend to take you kayaking on a smooth green creek. Then try it solo.
- Hop on the back of your husband's motorcycle. Maybe you'll want one of your own.
- Tried riding a bicycle lately? New models let you sit up straight and brake with your feet, just like you did when you were a girl.

Mary was a young wife in Hawaii when she decided to teach herself how to ride a surfboard. Her husband, an avid surfer, was overseas and Mary wanted to surprise him when he came home. "I'd always heard that surfers waxed their boards," says Mary, sheepishly explaining that she set to waxing her surfboard, using floor wax. "See, I thought they waxed their board so they could slip through the water faster. The real reason they wax their board is to get traction so they don't fall off. I'm from Arkansas. What did I know about surfing?"

Mary never launched her slippery board. "I'd almost get up on one side and then I'd slip off the other. Of course, I was too humiliated to ask anyone for help. I never tried it again." She switched to body surfing and that's what she's done for decades with her family, now two grown sons and grandsons. But for her sixty-third birthday, Mary's sons sent her to surfing camp in Santa Cruz, California.

"At the camp they guarantee that you'll stand up. But at my age the hard part is jumping on the board and landing on your knees. Finally I did get on and I got up," the instructor riding tandem next to her. "I got a minute's ride. I finally got the sense of standing up on top of the water and riding to shore. I understood this great feeling of freedom that they talk about. I was smiling the whole time and shrieking. When it was over I jumped up and shouted hooray."

She's back to body surfing, which she says "you can do forever. Age doesn't have anything to do with water. If you can catch the wave you can soar into the shore. I'm not as flexible as I used to be, but I feel the same as ever. Anyone can see I'm of grandmother age. I don't have to worry about being thirty and looking cool in my bikini."

Mary's mainstay is a utilitarian Speedo in navy blue. The last time she ordered one, there were no navy blue suits in her size and she was forced to buy purple. "My son said, 'Way to go, Mom.'"

Frequent Flyer

"They told me to let go of the bar. There was no way in hell I was going to let go. How did I ever get myself into this?" That was Jeannie Schulz's first experience, at fifty-six, on the flying trapeze. She was at a Club Med and stopped to watch when she saw a number of people lining up in front of a trapeze. "I started asking what they were doing, they assured me it was simple and I would be told what to do at the top of the ladder. Suddenly, it was my turn and I had to go up the ladder. It was about ten feet high, not much more than a household ladder, but I was scared to turn around and go back. I'd been talking to all these people and didn't want to embarrass myself.

- White-water river rafting gets the heart rate up. Go with a guide, get soaked, scream a lot. Or try skydiving. Make your kids go with you.
- Sign up for improvisational acting. You will never again be at a loss for words.
- Run for office.
- Go on record. Tell the city council or the newspaper editor what you think.
- Move to a different zip code. Your friends will visit.
- Travel alone for a week by train in a foreign country.
- Look up your high school sweetheart.
- Play hooky from work and finish reading (or writing) that novel.

"I had to get from the ladder to the platform and someone hooked my belt into the lines and told me to grab the swinging bar. I had one hand on the bar but I didn't want to let go of the platform. I said, 'I can't.' But I did grab the bar with two hands and swung out and was hanging there. Finally I dropped down into the net and crawled away, feeling like a total failure."

It was a while before Jeannie ventured near a trapeze again, although it bugged her that "other people could do it, so why couldn't I?" She'd think about it when she'd go to the park with her grandkids and would play around on the monkey bars. Then Jeannie met Sam Keen, the author-philosopher who has a personal trapeze setup in Sonoma, California, and first got into flying when he was sixty.

His platform is about thirty feet high and the net is eight feet off the ground. "There were a lot of younger people there," says Jeannie. "I was the slowest of them all. But they were really nice to me and offered encouragement."

It took her all one summer to accomplish a knee-hang, which involves flipping over the bar and hanging upside down. Coincidentally, the day she mastered the trick a network TV crew was present filming a feature story on Keen and captured Jeannie doing her debut knee-hang. The piece ran without mentioning that the daring middle-aged woman on the flying trapeze was the wife of Peanuts cartoonist Charles Schulz. Jeannie appreciated that, since the trapeze was her thing and had nothing to do with her famous husband, who preferred golf.

"I kept going back to Sam's because they were really encouraging, but I'd get butterflies in my stomach driving over there." It became a weekly thing, to climb the ladder, grab the swinging bar, and jump. Five or six times a session. Then it became twice a week. "I think at first it was sheer stubbornness to prove I could do it. Driving home each time I felt like I'd taken drugs. It was such an adrenaline rush."

The physical challenge and mental concentration also helped Jeannie get through her husband's illness and death. "It was a place I could be where nobody spent a lot of time talking.

They knew who I was, but the sociability and teamwork were around the trapeze. Once you're there you're simply focused. I needed that."

Trapeze work, she says, is not about strength but timing. "As you're swinging through the air, there is a point where you become weightless and that's when you do something," like grab another bar or do a somersault. "I'm not particularly poetic about it. To me, it's a whole new level of concentration at my advanced age. It's a pleasure to learn a new skill and to overcome fear. It's always good to be doing something better when you are sixty than you did at thirty."

Celebrate Yourself,
Go Shopping

There is no way to put a good spin on *matronly*, unless you are consciously wanting to tell the world, "Don't look at me. Go away. Just let me crawl under this gray prison garb and disappear." *Matronly* calls up images of shapeless, unremarkable garments designed to cover the body and never to enhance. There is no "matronly" section in any fashion boutique. It is not a look most of us are hoping to achieve.

However, the opposite of matronly can be as deadly. As in low-rise, belly-exposing pants. Tiny underwear shirts. The clothes you admire on daring young women, the ones more likely to pull it off without someone thinking, "Poor dear."

The very funny and knowing fashion guru Brenda Kinsel, author of *Brenda's Bible: Escape Fashion Hell and Experience Heaven Every Time You Get Dressed, 40 Over 40,* and other wardrobe guides, offers a regular fashion watch on her Web site. One feature on the site, titled "What Was She Thinking?" is a form of that favorite bitchy sport women know as "rating other women."

BETTER THAN A MIRROR

Not everyone can afford a personal image consultant, but we all have trusted friends who know what you mean when you ask if your back fat is showing. And who will kindly remind you that beige is no longer your best color.

Here are some hints some friends and I put together one night over mojitos in Key West on what to avoid and what to embrace over fifty:

- There's a thin line between looking eccentric and foolish, and it may change depending on where you live. What's amusing in California may have them calling the cops in Ohio.

- Go easy on the windbreakers and white tennis shoes. It's fine to look like a tourist when you are one, but you don't have to look like you just got off the bus.

- Baseball caps, yes. Tractor hats, no.

- Young women in warmup suits look like they're going to the gym. Older women look like they're going for a nap. Plus, the thick fabric plays hell with hot flashes.

- If you see yourself in a photo you don't like, rip up the photo and then consider ditching the outfit.

- A T-shirt dress with flowers on steroids is not meant to be worn away from the beach.

- Establish a signature item. A gold necklace you buy for yourself at a really good jewelry store. Your mother's diamond tennis bracelet. Cowboy boots.

- Don't dress to match your daughter, your husband, or your dog.

- Give yourself a break on hot, muggy days and go sleeveless. The twenty-five-year-old at the next table will be too consumed by her own flabby-arm worries to even notice yours.

- Everything looks better with a fresh attitude and lipstick to match.

One example Brenda cites is a mother and daughter in matching athletic shoes, drop-waist jeans, and cropped sweaters, mommy's tummy exposed just as much as her teenager's, to which Brenda groans, "What was she thinking?" On the flip side, she regularly gives raves to women who make her look twice, with pleasure, like the ninety-something "style maven" she spied in a pink jacket with a pink and white polka-dot skirt.

As for matronly clothes, or what Brenda also calls "dowdy and dumpy" and what my sister calls "henny," at the top of the list is a stiff A-line denim skirt with pleats in the front. Avoid them like the plague, says Brenda. My friend Sara would agree. She has a recurring nightmare in which she is part of a group of elderly women getting off a bus to go to the restroom at some desert stop, and she and the rest are wearing shapeless denim skirts.

Also making Brenda's matronly list are themed sweatshirts with sweatpants. "Decorated sweatshirts with matching pull-on pants are a great idea for toddlers but not for grown women," she writes in *40 Over 40*. Basically, "anything that resembles clothes for kids" should be avoided, she says. "Like those shapeless jumpers that make you look seven. And pregnant." (The day after we talked I dispatched my shapeless black jumper to the thrift store.)

Brenda says no to wearing sheer hose under your jeans. She doesn't mean winter tights under jeans, which are necessary for survival in the snow. But thin nylons? Instant old lady, she warns.

We do get to wear jeans forever, she says, although they require updating. "Watch out for ones that give you a butt that looks real wide and long. A lower-rise jean (not a super low rise) can cut that long rear view pant line by a few inches and make you look trimmer and younger. Also, those very narrow pant legs that come in at the ankle make the butt look wider yet. Don't let your ancient jeans make you look ancient, too."

Here's a challenge: is there any clothing item that older women look better in than younger women? Brenda answers yes. "We can wear expensive things better. Maybe not every woman will do furs because of the political issue, but I saw a wonderful mink poncho on an older woman

WHAT'S GOOD ABOUT GETTING OLDER?

Every woman will have her favorite answer to this question. Oh, come on. Yes, you do. Just think about it for a second. Here's a start.

- You've learned by now to value your time and spend it with people you enjoy—no whiners, backstabbers, or energy suckers.

- You don't have to be nice and go to baby showers, retirement dinners, or lingerie parties given by and for people you don't really like.

- As part of a large demographic of sympathetic women, you can count on there being at least one other guest at the party who will want the window open.

- You realize that there are times when you enjoy being invisible, when you can run into the grocery store in a baseball cap and no makeup, confident that no one will pay attention to you.

at an airport. Young people can't pull off luxuriousness the way older women can. Like cashmere lounge wear. Yummy stuff. Also grown-up, important jewelry, diamonds mixed with semiprecious stones."

Fashion is a crucial choice for women after fifty, says Brenda, a way to enjoy this next adventure or give up. Either women decide at this point to disappear because—what the hell—no one's looking at them anymore and they might as well put on this old schmatta. Or they open themselves and their wardrobes to all possibilities.

"This is the time to at last discover yourself, to express who you are. To throw yourself around. If not now, when?" she says. "Women after fifty potentially have more time and more money. They're doing their second or third career. They have an energy they can grab hold of. We can rediscover that passion for fashion that we had in our teenage years. We have more time to shop with friends. It can be a very creative time."

It's so important to not become invisible. As we get older the hair and skin change colors, maybe you lose some eyebrows and eyelashes, the skin is uneven in tone. It all contributes to blurriness. Nothing is defined. So this is the time for a woman to learn to apply makeup. To have an eyebrow line, a lip line is a way to not become invisible."

Another way, she says, is "to dabble in trends. Not head-to-toe trends, but to keep pace with the world." One approach is to shop the accessory department. "Look at the incidental pieces that come out every season. A poncho or shawl, scarf or belt in fashion colors. We can definitely do those things."

Think color. How much black is there in your closet? "This is a time to celebrate life and one way is to do it in your wardrobe. Clothes are such a wonderful vehicle because we can instantly get a different feeling about ourselves. I saw a woman sitting at a bar in a yellow leather jacket and that said to me, 'Here's a woman who knows how to have fun.'"

Lastly, says Brenda, who has had her share of downturns, including breast cancer, along with her successes, "Don't save anything for good. Good is right now."

- You get to have sex in the afternoon with no kids barging in.
- You have friends who will defend you and come to your immediate aid even if you become a vegan or join the NRA.
- You've developed such a network that if you move to Chicago or Berlin someone will give you a number to call.
- You recognize bullshit.
- You have survived teenagers, aging parents, multiple downturns in the economy, dubious mammograms, and the half-century mark. You are unstoppable.

"Why not seize the pleasure at once? How often is happiness destroyed by preparation, foolish preparation?" —jane austen

WHAT'S NOT SO GOOD ABOUT GETTING OLDER?

- You talk more about cholesterol than about orgasms.

- Your body is changing as fast as it did in adolescence, but backwards.

- You have an appointment for a mammogram, bone density scan, and colonoscopy, and none of these is as much fun as shoe shopping.

- You remember that silver dress in the Paris boutique that you decided was too young for you. And you were only forty at the time, for God's sake. What were you thinking?

- You can't remember your ATM number, your e-mail password, or what reminder you were going to write down on that yellow sticky note.

Here Come the Brides

When she was a college student in Kansas in the 1960s, Pauline, an artist, vowed never to marry. "I wanted adventure and travel. The only thing I thought that might work would be if I married some guy in the Navy and he'd be gone a lot and then we'd have romantic reunions in different places in the world."

That was back before feminism had convinced young women that they didn't have to marry at twenty-one like their mothers. And even though Pauline had the desire to be single, her parents believed she should marry, and as soon as possible.

"Basically, my mother told me I wasn't that pretty. Not that smart. My father didn't have that much money. So I better marry the first man who asked me."

Pauline married a motorcycle racer. "I decided that was kind of close to adventure. But mostly it meant going to hot summer fairs in the Midwest." The marriage lasted four years. "I said no more of that and focused on adventure and relationships that wouldn't tie me down."

For ten years she fished from her own salmon boat in the Pacific. "I loved fishing so much. Who needs a man? I thought. I was surrounded by men." She had a tubal ligation so she wouldn't have to worry about becoming pregnant. "You can't be thirty-five and have a baby and run a fishing boat."

Then she reconnected with a younger guy named John, a friend from college. They were both artists, had the same taste in music, and enjoyed a similar wacky humor. After college, Pauline had had her motorcycle marriage and John had married, fathered two kids, and eventually divorced. When he and Pauline hooked up again, she started living in a trailer on his Kansas property one summer. When she moved to California he followed. They would be short-term roommates and sometimes lovers and then go their separate ways. They talked about one day living together, when they were very old.

"When you're young you don't really think about growing old and being alone," says Pauline. "You like your freedom. You like bouncing around. If one guy drives you nuts you find a new boyfriend."

They almost married when Pauline was fifty-six, inviting guests from around the country to their wedding and naming attendants. The week before, they called off the wedding but had a party anyhow, with champagne and an already ordered wedding cake.

They continued their on-again, off-again relationship even after John moved to Massachusetts and Pauline stayed in California. Seven years later they decided they were ready to try again. She explains her turnaround. "I realized I could spend my life alone, and suddenly I didn't like that prospect. Now I realize what a narcissist I've always been. It has always been me first. My parents used to tell me I was unwilling to compromise, that I wanted what I wanted when I wanted it. And I guess they were right. But now I appreciate this super-nice man and I don't feel like being so self-absorbed. It's different being married and knowing you can't just get pissed and call it off every time things don't go your way. I like it much better this way. Of course, it took a few lonely dark winters to realize it."

Part of the reason they put off marriage was John's desire to be with his children. He moved whenever and wherever his ex-wife moved so he could be in proximity to his sons. And Pauline, who'd never been a mother, felt like she was always in second place behind his kids. "But now I think it was pretty admirable for him to stay with his kids until they finished high school. I once read an advice columnist who said you know you're ready to marry when you feel confident enough in yourself to achieve some perspective on the person you're marrying."

They had a small wedding in Todos Santos in Baja, Mexico, where they've since bought a house on a hill, with a view of the ocean. For now they're living together in California, but they intend to eventually move to Mexico for good. John will create his metal sculptures and Pauline will make her art. It wasn't what her parents had in mind, but Pauline finally did end up with the man and the house. Forty years later.

Love Is Lovelier

Kat, mother of two, became a bride for the second time at age fifty-six to Michael, fifty-one. She wore white lace and he wore a pink rose in his lapel. The ceremony was held near a lake in the woods in New Hampshire, a place where her father's family had vacationed every summer. The nuptial couple had planned an idyllic summer weekend, with guests swimming, sailing, canoeing, and playing tennis on the lovely clay courts in the piney woods.

Instead, they had three solid days of freezing rain. So they adjusted their plans, which is easier to do at fifty-six than it is at twenty-six. "We doubled our wine order," says Kat, "and all these wonderful people put on every scrap of summer clothing they had brought and huddled together in the cottages, throwing log after log on the fires and drinking bottle after bottle of wine and just talking to each other and singing songs. They said they had the best time ever had at a wedding. Me, too."

A Boston-based writer, Kat now spends her weekends riding on her husband's motorcycle and riding horses on vacation. For their honeymoon she and Michael went to Ireland and rode horses every day for a week. Marriage, she says, has brought much adventure to her life.

What also surprises Kat about marriage in her fifties is that "it's possible to get really, really angry with your spouse and even almost hate him awhile, and then to truly get past it and move on and feel even more loving than before. I didn't know that in my first marriage."

My Boyfriend's Back

Dennis and Pat were high school sweethearts in Ypsilanti, Michigan, in the 1960s. In her prom picture Pat has a pile of sausage curls on top of her head. Dennis played in a band called the Del Shays. Can't you just taste the onion dip and cherry Cokes? They went to drive-in movies, she wore his ring on a chain around her neck, and they spent so much time together at their Catholic school that the worried nuns alerted Pat's mother.

After high school graduation Pat lived at home and went to the local college. Dennis enlisted in the Air Force. Pat wrote every day, but the distance between them and the many lonely weekends eventually got to her, and she married someone else.

The two didn't see each other for more than thirty years. And then in 2000 Pat went to a high school reunion and ran into Dennis's brother, who reported that Dennis had briefly married but was currently single. So, after two marriages, was Pat.

"After the reunion I couldn't get Dennis out of my mind. My daughter kept telling me, 'Call him, Mom. What's the worst that can happen?'" So she did call him, and Dennis came home one day to hear a familiar sweet, flat Michigan voice on his answering machine. He poured himself a beer and called back. They talked for two hours that night, and again the next night, and they began e-mailing three and four times a day. Soon he invited her to fly to Reno and meet him for a little Western vacation.

"It was so thrilling, like getting asked to the prom," says Pat. At the airport, they recognized each other immediately. "We walked through the airport arm in arm like we'd never parted," she says.

Dennis told her that he was "scared as hell" and that if it didn't work out he was going to join an order of monks. But it did work out. Pat quit her job as a lawyer, sold her house in Detroit, and moved to California. They married. Soon afterward, Dennis lost his job of twenty-four years with a computer company, so they packed up and moved to Florida. When you find true love at fifty-four, you're not afraid of starting over.

Carol Finds Love Online

Carol started working as a therapist and grief counselor when the AIDS epidemic hit the San Francisco Bay Area in 1985. She spent a lot of time holding the hands of dying young men and cursing their killer. She retired at sixty to become a reading teacher and enjoy a quiet, solo life with her two cats. But then she discovered love online. This is how her romance grew, as reported in abbreviated e-mail bulletins from Carol to her friends:

> Hi. I've hit pay dirt online. We have been e-mailing and phoning for two months. She's sixty-one and we both have been alone for about the same amount of time. One of the teachers at school has been witnessing how much fun I am having and decided to go online, too. It's the newest way of meeting someone and it works. —Love, Carol

Hi. Met with K, the woman I've been doing online communication with. Yep . . . it's a potential relationship. She is a very grounded and wonderful woman. Kind, gentle, strong, outdoorsy, a hiker. Have lots in common. Jazz, good conversation, intelligent. We will begin meeting every third week and build toward becoming partners. I am still rather in shock, didn't expect this to happen. I am ready. She thinks I am the woman of her dreams. Well, I hope so. —Love, Carol

Hi. Lesbians are famous for meeting, falling in love, crawling into the sack with each other, moving in . . . and moving out! I fell in love with K way before we ever saw each other physically. Having the freedom to get to know each other online through writing feelings and thoughts was a great help. When we did meet and first lay eyes on each other, all the important questions had been answered. We spent the weekend in blissful lovemaking, reading poetry to each other, going for walks holding hands and kissing behind trees, dancing to Etta James's "At Last" and just adoring each other. We felt so lucky that we had found each other. —Love, Carol

Hi. I have made a definite decision to leave Santa Rosa [California] and move to be with my love. It's been interesting to tell people and watch them freak out. "So soon, don't you think you should wait a year?" I respond, "Hey . . . wake up, she's sixty-one, I'm sixty-six. What the hell do we want to wait for . . . to get older? She sent me an e-mail saying, in part, "Hopefully, dying in our sleep on the trip to celebrate our thirtieth anniversary is where our story together will end." I mean, how could I not fall in love with someone with such courage? As much courage as I have. —Love, Carol

Hi. I am overwhelmed and amazed that at sixty-six I will probably have more fun having sex than ever before in my life. I have always been a sexual person, but for so many years my feelings were covered with shame and a disease called homophobia that I internalized. Along with my journey of learning about life and death has come my continued ownership of my right to be a sensual/sexual person on this planet. It is my right and something I will never feel shame about again. —Love, Carol

Hi. My friends Wes and his partner Steve are having a going-away party for me. Kathy and I will leave the next day for Idyllwild [in Southern California]. I have no doubts that as older women we have every skill needed to have a great, fun-filled life together . . . and it's about damn time for both of us. —Love, Carol

Happily Single

We don't call them "old maids" anymore. In the twenty-first century we call them "single"—got a problem with that? Sociologist Kay Trimberger documented a new trend: unmarried women who are not only content but also happy with their single status in her book *The New Single Woman.* The university professor and never-married mother of an adult son became a professional expert on the subject as she did research for her book.

The Berkeley, California, author has lived the life, experiencing "the long conflicted process in society towards singleness," and can report that singles are successfully challenging the stereotype "that you need to be coupled to be happy." That doesn't mean that society has caught up with the notion. Remember the *Sex and the City* episode when Candice Bergen is afraid to be dateless at her own party?

Still, there are plenty of positive role models, says Kay, that demonstrate to young women (and their mothers) that single is a viable alternative to marriage and not the booby prize.

A little over a third of American women in their fifties are single, according to U.S. Census figures. Not all are giddy about their status, but there are plenty who feel just fine with their arrangement, says Kay. In her research she found that those who don't spend most of their time focused on finding a partner, "but rather build the structural supports for a viable life," are more likely to be happy single women.

The things that make single women feel good about their lives, she found, are some of the same things that make married women happy, including having their own home, meaningful work, network of friends and family. "To defend being single is not to be against marriage. I say that being coupled is great and being single is great and we should have cultural support for both."

In many ways, she found, the single woman's life is not that different from her married friends' lives. She says that if more people realized this and considered singleness just another choice, they wouldn't marry out of desperation. The better-adjusted single women had established a network of friends, family members, and traveling companions. They were active in political groups, social clubs, churches, and sports. They also had developed "new connections to the next generation" by caring for their own children or nieces and nephews, mentoring younger colleagues at work, or volunteering to spend time with young people.

MAINTAINING YOUR SINGLE BLISS

The single women in Kay Trimberger's study who were most contented shared the following characteristics:

- Each has a nurturing home.
- Her work is satisfying.
- She's comfortable with her sexuality, in both style and level of activity.
- She connects with the next generation.
- She finds emotional intimacy with friends and family.
- She participates in her community.

As for romance, one of Kay's goals has been "to combat the idea that romance is the only route to happiness or adventure." Again, it's part of the culture. Single people are always being asked about their love life. Married people aren't. Kay answers that a lot of singles enjoy their celibacy, just as many have very active sexual lives "without the need or expectation of romantic love."

In the 1980s, when she was forty, Kay adopted her son. She found other parents, both singles and couples, to discuss child-raising questions with. "I had many friends to bounce things off. I never felt isolated." That's one thing that single women do well, she says. "We are good at creating networks and developing extended family."

Kay has her home, friends, continued teaching possibilities, her new book. Last year she went to Peru with ten friends. Her now-grown son lives nearby. She has what makes her happy, including economic security and a community of both singles and couples, two factors that play a significant role in a happy single life. She now even has the silverware that her mother had been saving for years for her wedding gift.

Looking for Jill and the Gang in the Movies

Many of us are grateful to Jill Clayburgh for transforming a T-shirt and underpants into sexy sleepwear. After seeing *An Unmarried Woman* in 1978 I gave up, once and for all, any attempt to wear anything with frills or feathers to bed and opted instead for the comfortable combo worn by Jill's character, Erica. She was our kind—a member of that generation of partially liberated women undone by divorce but coming back with confidence, and maybe a bushy-faced Alan Bates–type lover on the side. Like *Sex and the City* would do a generation later, *An Unmarried Woman* offered a pretty valid snapshot of women in their thirties living in New York, sharing their hopes and disappointments, openly discussing bad men and good sex. No wonder we identified with Jill, even if we didn't live in New York and would never look as cute as she did while pirouetting to the music of *Swan Lake* in her skivvies.

A generation of women now in their fifties and beyond grew older along with Jill Clayburgh, Candice Bergen, Diane Keaton, Jacqueline Bisset, Julie Christie, and Jane Fonda. There was a whole slew of clever, attractive film stars who were members of our club, agewise at least. Some you still see. Some you don't. They were our contemporaries, even though we'd never look as good in a close-up or have movie sex with Robert Redford. But they portrayed our changing world. As they got older, we got older, and when Hollywood started to pass over actresses who represented us, or relegated them to bitchy mother-in-law or crazy landlady roles, we took it personally.

In her fifties Jill Clayburgh appeared in *Never Again,* a film about a disheartened divorced mother whose daughter leaves for college. It's a good "girly night" film to rent when you're feeling cranky but needing a reason to hope. Her character, Grace, is living through another culturally confusing time. She and her wickedly funny New York friends lament the middle-age dating scene, the lack of sex, and their annoyance at how Hollywood ignores women over thirty-five. The only time a woman that age has sex in a movie, they grouse, is right before she gets decapitated.

Sad truth, agrees Jill Clayburgh. Older women are still not very well represented in the movies, she says, and tells me about being turned down for a TV sitcom role in which she would have played the mother of twenty-year-olds. It didn't matter to the producers, she says, that she was then the real-life mother of twenty-year-olds. "They told me I was fifteen years too old to play the part." Broadway's different. In 2005 she returned to New York's theater scene in two plays.

MOVIES THAT KNOW HOW TO TREAT A TOMATO*

*In which the un-young women sometimes enjoy great sex, are appealing and interesting, and, even if they're unapologetically bitchy, make us like them, if only because they transcend the middle-age stereotype.

Afterglow—Julie Christie as Phyllis Mann, former B-movie actress obsessed with a visiting contractor.

Autumn Tale—Béatrice Romand as Magali, a widow and wine producer, and Marie Rivière as Isabelle, her best friend who decides to find Magali a new husband.

The Clearing—Helen Mirren has to deliver the ransom for her husband, Robert Redford, held captive by an employee.

The Divine Secrets of the Ya-Ya Sisterhood—Ellen Burstyn as sensitive Southern mother to Sandra Bullock, a playwright who has angered her mother by her comments in a magazine interview. So many good women—Maggie Smith, Fionnula Flanagan, Shirley Knight—as Burstyn's friends, intervene.

84 Charing Cross Road—Anne Bancroft as Helen Hanff, a feisty New York writer who begins a touching and humorous correspondence with reserved English bookseller Anthony Hopkins that lasts two decades.

Indochine—Catherine Deneuve in Indochina during the 1930s as French colonialist Elaine, owner of a large rubber-tree plantation, a proud and imprudent woman who lives with her father and her adoptive native daughter.

The Lion in Winter—Katharine Hepburn as the bitter and brilliant imprisoned Queen Eleanor of Aquitaine at Christmastime, 1183, when her aging husband King Henry II, played by Peter O'Toole, plans a reunion with their three sons and his mistress to name his successor.

Moonlight Mile—Susan Sarandon, playing a writer who, with husband played by Dustin Hoffman, must deal with her daughter's fiancé after the young woman is killed in a car crash.

Mother—Anne Reid is a recent widow and grandmother who has a passionate affair with a man half her age who is also sleeping with her daughter.

Mrs. Brown—Judi Dench's extraordinary portrayal of Queen Victoria after being widowed, and her complex relationship with John Brown, a simple Scottish Highlander.

Never Again—Professional woman and mother Jill Clayburgh, whose daughter has just left for college, vows never to fall in love again, until she meets Jeffrey Tambor at a gay bar, tapping into long-forgotten feelings they both had thought were gone forever.

Robin and Marian—Autumn romance with Audrey Hepburn as older Maid Marian who, now in a convent, meets up with older Robin, Sean Connery.

Room at the Top—Simone Signoret as an unhappily married French actress with a theatrical troupe in a dreary English factory town who has caught the eye of younger man Laurence Harvey, who is scheming to have both his young fiancée and the older actress.

A Rumor of Angels—Vanessa Redgrave as an old woman in Maine who helps a young boy resolve his feelings over the death of his mother.

Something's Gotta Give—Famous playwright Diane Keaton, divorced, has forsaken all love and romance until she meets full-time philanderer Jack Nicholson, who is dating her daughter.

Something to Talk About—Gena Rowlands as the mother of Julia Roberts, who discovers that her husband is cheating on her and comes to live with her sister, only to receive the advice of her mother, wanted or not.

Terms of Endearment—Shirley MacLaine, as strong, irritating, loving mother to dying Debra Winger, becomes paramour to flaky ex-astronaut Jack Nicholson.

Under the Sand—Charlotte Rampling's husband disappears during a vacation in France and she is left to reflect on the mystery of her marriage and her future.

The Winter Guest—Phyllida Law as the mother to real-life daughter Emma Thompson, who plays Frances, a recent widow who wants to get away from Scotland to escape her memories.

She quickly adds that it's not exclusively Hollywood's problem. "You can't just mourn the lack of movie roles without mourning how society values women past fifty. Maybe when the Madeleine Albrights take over, things will change. But movies reflect society."

It's complex, she says. "Celluloid is a very plastic medium. Movies are not the theater, where there are great roles for women. A lot of film is about the beauty of things. The way the camera rolls over that leaf. The way it focuses on fresh, dewy skin, which is very nice to look at. Movies are the realm of those with beautiful flesh." On the other hand, she mentions seeing a contemporary perform in a play and noticing that "she had this big, beautiful forehead which didn't move. Botox doesn't look very good on actresses. Give me a face with expression. Give me a Judi Dench face, a Maggie Smith."

Eschewing life in California, Jill Clayburgh lives with her playwright husband David Rabe in Connecticut. "I couldn't live in Hollywood," she says. "I would feel like the oldest one working there. It's a really aberrant society, the hysteria over looking young, all the Botox. It's very distorted."

She believes, however, that aesthetics are changing in regard to what's beautiful. For example, she says, "I had an interesting reaction when Eileen Fisher started using older models. I didn't embrace it immediately. Intellectually I did, but I didn't know if I liked the look. Now I think it's beautiful. That educated me, even though I thought that I was already educated."

There are other slow improvements, she thinks. "When I was growing up, thirty was considered old. I remember when Ali McGraw turned thirty and everyone was horrified. How could Ali McGraw be thirty? Now, thirty is no longer considered over the hill."

As for keeping herself in shape at age sixty, the actress relies on "good genes from two tall, thin parents. That's 90 percent of it. The rest comes from working out. I get off work and I go on the Stairmaster. It's my mental relaxation. I love the feeling of my body in motion. Take me to the beach, I'll jump in the water."

On aging, she says, "Lying about your age doesn't work. Maybe you can buy a couple of years by lying, but pretty much people look their age. They might look really good for their age but they still look their age."

One of the actress's friends is a wise, older artist who lives nearby in Connecticut. "She is so sharp. She makes huge sculptures and has such a positive life force. I see parts of people all the time who I admire, who I would want to be. Their minds are still being challenged. They have enthusiasm and interest in life. Even if they are physically compromised, they don't whine. I hate whining."

Une Femme D'un *Certain Age*

The French are credited with creating the phrase "women of a certain age," although they are charmingly vague about when that age begins and ends. American novelist Diane Johnson, who has contributed to the mythology and appeal of French women in her books, including *Le Divorce,* thinks that "a certain age" means "over forty until an indefinite older age. It seems to imply, past first youth but still in the game."

Diane, who has homes in Paris and San Francisco, is not only a chronicler of modern French life from an American perspective but also an observer of the differences between French and American women. In her novel *L'Affaire,* the main character, a rich dot-com executive from Silicon Valley, describes mature Parisian women as "the essence of France" . . . "animated, slender people in suits, the perfumed women carrying perfect handbags."

As for what American women might learn from French women about presentation, Diane says, "I think French women can teach us that you have to spend more money on clothes as you get older, and you should never hesitate to go to a nice restaurant by yourself if you feel like it and order a great dinner and some wine. It helps if, as in France, the society respects older women, but it's a circular process. It's a cliché, but we have to feel good about ourselves, and that means looking good in a suitable way—not embarrassing attempts at youth. French women don't do that, but they do all have blonde hair after a certain age."

If you read Diane Johnson's novels you also know that French women of all ages make it a priority to invest in expensive, sexy underwear.

Asked to describe how the quintessential middle-aged French woman puts herself together, Diane says, "She wears a suit, scarf, and jewelry, earrings always, and a nifty new handbag. She doesn't necessarily have a lot of clothes, but good ones."

As they age, French women can also enjoy an important role in the family, says Diane. "The importance of the extended family secures a spot for the older woman as matriarch. I'm sure there's friction but it also gives a role. French kids don't have school on Wednesdays, so grandmothers often step in and spend the day with their grandchildren, another useful role.

"Also, the convention is that women remain attractive later than American men seem to believe. Women are liked more by men in France. So French women have the advantage."

Evelyne, fifty-four, a teacher in Orleans in the Loire Valley, says she and her French friends don't feel the need to lie about their age. "That would sound coquettish and ridiculous," she says. Her mother's generation, however, felt differently. "As children we were told never to ask someone's age. If asked, my mother would say she was eighteen." Evelyne and her friends believe that "it's stupid to try to mimic youth."

Also, there's something more useful to cultivate besides looks, she says. "Beauty is important but I think at our age what we call 'charme' prevails." That includes "curiosity for life, paying attention, giving a warm welcome and a good smile."

Her friend Benedicte, also a teacher, concurs. "Charm is more important than beauty. It's an alchemy of intelligence, spirit, a capacity for love and tenderness, honesty, lucidity, and joie de vivre."

Anna, an American, moved to the French countryside in her fifties to teach English, study French, and write short stories. Right off she noticed women's attention to fashion, even in her small Burgundy village. "Casual dress here isn't as casual as it is in America. French women's bras are wired and lacy. The necklines are frequently low and the shoes are often strapped, narrow, and with a skinny heel. They don't wear running pants or sweatshirts." Anna also notes that, no matter where she travels in France, "I seem to be the only woman my age with gray hair."

Even so, Anna enjoys attention from French men. "I don't get nods from men in America, but I do here. Age or size seems to make little difference to French men. French men give all women a nod of recognition, so I don't think women feel as invisible in France as in America."

AND ON WE GO

We are the generation that said we want more and helped open the sky to women. And so we big sisters, great-aunts, mothers, and grandmothers continue the momentum, demonstrating the charm, wisdom, and grit of midlife and beyond. We didn't get this far to say this is enough. The adventure doesn't end when you know you've got the juice.

They used to say—

- They used to say that women over thirty-five shouldn't wear their hair long.
- They used to say women over forty-five shouldn't show bare arms.
- They used to say all women over fifty better dye their hair and lie about their age.
- They used to say after baby-making women had nothing more to contribute.
- They used to say that menopausal women couldn't be world leaders.
- "They" didn't know we'd stopped listening.

PART TWO

Living Juicy

Move to Mexico, Open an Inn

When she was forty-eight Dianne Kurshner bought a two-hundred-year-old house in San Miguel de Allende in northern central Mexico. A year later she had turned it into an inn, the Casa Luna—"short for *lunatica* (lunatic)," she says with a laugh. "When I opened the door for business I had $150 left in the world." She also points out that *luna* (the moon) is "a feminist symbol for change," which is what she wanted and what she got.

The first Casa Luna became so successful that she opened a second inn a block away, giving her a total of twenty-six rooms.

Alone, she created a new business and a new life in a foreign country—a single American woman in a male-dominated Latin culture. With little Spanish vocabulary and few friends in town she had to learn how to do business and go about remodeling her old Spanish colonial building using Mexican laborers and local building techniques.

Now the former Californian has a sprawling, bright rooftop apartment in the middle of downtown San Miguel, two dogs who join her guests for margarita hour, a savvy bilingual, bicultural manager, and lots of business. Her inns are regularly listed in vacation guides and food and travel magazines.

In her prior life Dianne was a psychotherapist and a graphic designer of tabletop books. Before that, she was a ski bum at Lake Tahoe and a blackjack dealer. Then a high school friend was murdered in Los Angeles and two other friends died of cancer. "Three deaths in six months made me stop and evaluate what I was doing. It was time to change my life, take a risk, do something new in a new country. I really wanted an adventure." She'd visited San Miguel, a Spanish colonial town with cobblestone streets, when she was a college student in the 1970s and remembered it as being "filled with artists and eccentrics."

By the time she returned, San Miguel had already started becoming a popular lure for tourists and American and Canadian expatriates. Dianne started looking at real estate and dreaming of buying a fixer-upper and maybe starting a business. "I knew I had to have an income to live there. At the time there were only a couple of bed and breakfasts in town and the airport [ninety minutes away in Leon] had just opened up. I was right on the boom."

As a foreigner she couldn't get a Mexican bank loan, nor would an American bank lend money for a Mexican business. But she was lucky enough to buy her first building from a Texas couple who allowed her to make payments. "What I knew was that I didn't want to be a psychotherapist anymore. I love hearing people's stories but I have a hard time sitting still. I think I'm more of a creative type and entrepreneur."

One way she became known was by putting her inn on a popular San Miguel house-and-garden tour. "Sometimes I would stand at the door and say 'psst' to tourists walking by and invite them in. I started getting referrals. I had four rooms, then nine, then I developed a Web site."

Now she sees herself as a bridge between the two cultures. "The differences between Americans and Mexicans are big ones. For example, Americans are right on schedule and Mexicans have a different concept of time. I try to get the gringo tourists to slow down and get the Mexicans to understand that people need to catch a plane and must have breakfast on time. That's changed me. The lesson I learn every day is about patience and humility."

To her, being an expat means "I live out of the country," but she intends to hold on to her American citizenship. She's made some friends, both Mexican and American, but says, "it can be difficult to make close Mexican friends unless you marry into a family." As for dating, she advises other single women not to come to San Miguel looking for a husband. "There are plenty of men to flirt and dance with, but the joke among women here is if you meet an available man he's probably looking for a nurse or a purse."

Otherwise, she says, her town is "a good place for single women. It's safe, and there's plenty to do," including musical concerts, live theater, and so many art-show openings that you could go to one every night. And Mexican doctors make house calls, as do veterinarians. She can also get her favorite retinol cream over the counter at a fraction of the U.S. cost.

She stays in touch with American friends through e-mail and visits and keeps up with the news by watching the BBC and CNN and reading news online. She admits that she sometimes gets "a little tug in the heart" when she sees images of California in a movie or on TV. "But when I think about where else I would want to live I just don't have the answer."

"On the whole, age comes more gently to those who have some doorway into an abstract world—art, or philosophy, or learning—regions where the years are scarcely noticed and the young and old can meet in a pale truthful light."
—**freya stark,** travel adventure writer

Gypsy Woman

A lot of women like to think they have the soul of a gypsy, but how many dare to pack their bags and start down the road? What if you end up broke, unloved, and regretting that you gave up a boring but sure thing?

Author Meredith Blevins ran away in middle age and started writing novels, using her new life as research. Meredith, now in her early fifties, lives in the Four Corners area of the Southwest, a place loaded with natural wonders, ancestral magic, and characters. She doesn't have to look much beyond her front door or bathroom mirror for inspiration.

"I wanted to write books populated by women like me and like my friends—women who were aging and doing it with pizzazz," says Meredith. "I wanted my characters to be old enough to have gone through good and tough times with their kids and jobs and relationships. I have women write me regularly because not only is my main character still attractive and juicy, but so is her mother-in-law, a woman in her seventies.

"I wanted my characters to be resilient and textured, which only happens over time. I wanted them to have earned the right to their love affairs, their whims, and to know their own boundaries. Women characters who'd hold tight to their friends and their family members, to understand people are not disposable objects, and know you often love someone even though they drive you crazy. This is a way one decides to look at the world, and it colors all choices. This is true for my characters and for me. My main character is single; I'm not. If I didn't have a partner who was an ideal fit, I would be single."

Meredith, who has worked as a teacher, financial columnist, and music therapist, ran away from her home and steady job in California in 1998 in order to figure out what was next. It wasn't an easy choice.

"I knew I wanted to leave," says Meredith, "but I also had responsibilities, to my mom, eighty-six then, and to my kids, one in college, the other seventeen. It took a lot of juggling to make things work for everyone. We worked together; my mom and my daughter were a huge emotional support. The person who leaves had better be ready to kiss a lot of familiar comforts adios. Yes, it takes courage to leave. But [along with the] support from friends and family, [I had] a willingness to believe that, no matter what, I would be okay. Better than okay."

Searching for a place to start over, she tried out the Southwest, where her father had lived and where Meredith had spent time as a kid. Friends offered her their house in a little town in Utah for three months. "When I first arrived in this town of three hundred, I didn't know if I could make it through all three months. After one and a half months, I realized fate had conspired to carry me [to this, my] home. This place is a Southwestern version of *Northern Exposure* (the TV show), on the edge of Monument Valley. A mix of Anglos, Navajos, artists. Good people. In a town this size, you may not get along with everyone, but everyone is treasured."

She also brought her mother. "One of my prerequisites for deciding where to live was that it have a decent place for my mom. We had great times her last few years drinking Scotch and eating chocolate, bringing her the latest great-grandchild on her birthday. Making these kinds of arrangements can be tough when you hit the trail, but it can be done."

Meredith ended up marrying a man who also loves and writes about the Southwest, Win Blevins, a former journalist who had taken his own big leap to quit and write full-time. "I didn't expect to fall in love again. More than that, I didn't expect to find a partner who would see me and love me. But there it was and is—flab and all, we love each other. This kind of partnership would not have happened for either of us when we were younger. Taking care of each other, enjoying each other, just being together. What a gift time brings us in the awareness that none of us came with a warranty. We understand that this life doesn't last forever."

She also didn't expect to take to the wilds like she did. "I could never have imagined myself living in a place that takes five hours to get to the nearest large airport, two hours to the closest large supermarket. But in the city, I was bombarded with so much noise that I was unaware of how shut down my senses were. I like going back to the city, any area of population. [But] after four days, I feel like the kid who ate her chocolate Easter bunny in one hour—too much. Now I know the difference between a raven and a buzzard by the shape of their wings. I feel time as large and rippled, not as wristwatch time. I know how the sky smells if a sandstorm is heading our way. I can hear myself out here.

"It's living on the planet in a way that's part of it. It's not New Age thinking. Being who you were meant to be, taking your place in the tribe as that person, is a way of living that's as old as time. When I wake up now, most mornings look like they should, like a frigging miracle."

BEFORE YOU START PACKING

Loujean LaMalfa, a Northern California relocation consultant, published an award-winning business journal, *Living in Mexico: Updates and Business News*, and still gives talks to baby boomers on how to make Mexico their second home. For decades she's split her time in California and Puerto Vallarta, where she has enjoyed tamale trucks, concerts on the beach, safe walks at night, and a graceful Mexican pace. As nice as it sounds, she warns that a move out of the country is not for everyone.

Here's some of her advice:

- It's not like in the movies. If you're looking for a cheap villa and a man who will make love to you in a foreign language, it is better to go for the house, not the romance.

- Do your homework. Spend time investigating the good and bad points of a permanent move. Try to start planning three to five years out. Look into the boring legal and practical issues like car ownership and health care.

- Beware of books that say you can live on $500 a month. Your ability to make this happen depends on how far out of town you live and how much you like having running water and electricity.

- A foreigner can buy property in Mexico, but most deals are done on a cash-only basis.

- In places with large English-speaking populations, you don't necessarily have to be fluent in the local language to socialize. But remember that the housekeeper and the car mechanic will probably not speak English, nor will the clerk at the phone company. Even if you speak the language poorly, the effort is appreciated.

- Go native. It's hard to immerse yourself in the community, but it's easier if you study the culture, learn the language, and get involved by volunteering with a charitable organization, school, or bilingual library.

- Thinking about getting a job? Don't expect to make money, although if you have your own specialty, like tax preparation, or if you sell real estate or time-shares, you might be hired by a local company that needs your expertise.

- When you first move to a new country everything new is enchanting. Then reality sets in. You may find you dislike standing in long bank lines or living next to a church that sets off fireworks every saint's day.

- After about two to five years of living in another country many people start to get homesick. You miss your old friends, family, culture. You miss speaking English.

- Position yourself well. Be careful that you're not so isolated that you can't get to an airport and fly home in case of a family emergency.

- Don't give up on the home front until you are truly certain that a permanent move is what you really want. If you sell your home in the States and Mexico doesn't work out, you may have nothing to move back to.

- Mind your manners. Take a huge suitcase full of patience. Don't go to any country and start muttering, "Back in the States, we do it better." If you feel that way, go back to the States.

"All serious daring starts from within." —eudora welty

- Listen to yourself.

- When you hear your voice, do not settle for less than following it.

- There are so many possibilities out there.

- Running away from home doesn't necessarily mean running away from your mate. If you're lucky, your mate is your best pal. In that case, you can change your life together.

- Don't just think about what your grown kids are doing, or how close you want to live to them—they can move away at any time.

- Be willing to help your grown kids when they need emotional help or a place to stay, but set clear boundaries regarding how long they can squat. "You have both done the mother-and-child thing already," says Meredith. "You don't need to do the nurturing act with each other anymore. Instead, aim to be loving confidantes."

- Know that it is your turn.

Kick-Butt Women

Like most women, I know too many people who have been hammered by breast cancer. They are some of the funniest, happiest, relieved, grateful women I've ever met. I think they always did have a sense of humor, but they seem even more playful now. Is that what normally happens? When you get that close to the dark, do you end up developing your light side?

After chemotherapy Nancy took advantage of her bald head to become a Jack-o-Lantern for Halloween. She painted her head and face orange and colored a toilet-paper roll green to tape on top. Her son told her he wanted to get cancer when he grew up so he could paint his head too. Nancy told him he could shave and paint his head any time he wanted. So that Christmas her son and husband shaved their heads in solidarity and all three appeared bald in the family Christmas card.

I attended a dinner party for women who had met at a chemo center and were all at various stages of cancer. They hold these dinners every month and applaud each woman who walks in the door. Big cheers for the woman who was diagnosed eighteen years ago. And for the newly diagnosed who just got through a hellish week. And for the hostess, who always wears red and says that when things get scary, she drives around town blasting rock music in the middle of the night. At the dinner I mentioned writing a book about women's fears of getting older. It wasn't exactly their worry, they said. "We *want* to get old," roared one woman.

A few months later I met Dr. Jerri Nielsen, the doctor who was working at the South Pole when she discovered her own breast cancer. Like many people, I had followed her story in the media, the amazing accounts of how she did her own biopsy and administered her own chemo, to finally be airlifted from her research station. Jerri wrote a book about her experience, called *Ice Bound,* and Susan Sarandon played her in a movie. When I interviewed her I asked her what she thought interested people about her story. Jerri responded, "It's probably because I'm just like anybody, a middle-aged, overweight lady going on an adventure . . . [to live in the] highest, driest, coldest, windiest, and emptiest place on earth." At times she doubted that she'd live long enough to be rescued, yet she still recognized the value of her experience. "I wondered if my life would ever again feel so complete."

When we talked she was in the middle of a book tour and helping to raise money for breast cancer programs. She'd met a huge club of cancer survivors across the country. She called them "kick-butt women."

My friend Joan kicked butt. When I heard that she had been diagnosed with breast cancer, I screamed out, "That's it," as if it mattered to anyone that I was personally fed up with this wretched disease. I think of breast cancer as a stalker. A sadistic, mean son of a bitch with bad teeth who was probably unloved as a child. "No," I declared. That creep could have no more wonderful women.

But Joan took on the creep. She, who had found her lump while getting dressed after swimming at the Y, enlisted her husband to accompany her to every doctor's appointment. He took notes and recorded the discussions so they wouldn't miss a detail. After much thought, Joan decided to have her diseased breast removed and then chose to have the healthy one taken also, as a preventive measure. It was radical, she knew, but she didn't mind becoming flat chested. She said she had always thought her breasts were too big.

Her treatments made her tired and weak and sometimes confused. "I tell everybody I'm fine and then one I day I went in the house and left the car running with the keys inside for two hours. Finally a neighbor noticed." Wanting something to buffer the nausea from the chemo, she went to a clinic and bought medical marijuana. She appreciated that the clerks there called her "ma'am" and took credit cards. She said it felt like an act of defiance "to put marijuana on my Visa card."

An accomplished sculptor and jewelry designer, Joan took an art therapy class for cancer patients and added painting to her talents. On her sixtieth birthday she held an art show to celebrate her new paintings and the return of her curly black hair.

I once asked comic Lily Tomlin at a breast cancer benefit for her thoughts on using humor to fight disease. "It's the only way to take off that awful charge," she said, mentioning writer Norman Cousins, who said he had gotten through a life-threatening illness by watching Marx Brothers movies.

Women of another generation suffered in a different way because they had to hide. Breast cancer was a whispered diagnosis, a shameful subject. A woman missing a breast was considered incomplete. She felt that she had to hide her disfigurement. She did not cover her mastectomy scar with a redwood branch tattoo and show it proudly to her friends. She didn't climb mountains and go white-water rafting with other cancer survivors. She didn't proclaim her illness with a pink ribbon and a bald head. She certainly didn't make jokes.

It helps, Lily Tomlin said, "to speak the unspeakable. Sharing the frustration, the sense of the ridiculousness and the tragic, it binds you to others."

Patsy had a double mastectomy, which left her with drains dangling awkwardly from the incisions in her chest, until she hit upon the idea to contain them by wearing her husband's jock strap. When she showed her surgeon he cracked up.

My friend Annie walked into my living room in a blue hat, and before we could hug she said, "Okay, you want to get it over with?" and removed her hat. Hers was a lovely head, covered with pale down. "I think I have a nice neck," she said. I told her she also had big, gorgeous blue eyes and very straight, white teeth.

Minus her wispy blonde curls, you could see Annie's face better, but there were also other things to see—the dread, fear, loss, and sadness at getting the same damn disease as her mother and her sister. In summation she said, "It's been a big fucking drag, but I'm going to live." One morning after our walk she asked if I wanted to see her breast. She had finished radiation weeks before and said that at first she had looked pretty beat up. The breast was not misshapen, but I could see where the doctor had done a lumpectomy, under the nipple. The skin on her breast was light brown, as if it had been out in the sun too long, and it felt hotter than the other one.

Before Annie started her treatments she had gone to Mexico on a yoga and salsa-dancing retreat. Her doctor said there was no rush. Go have fun. When she started chemo she shaved her head rather than wait for the hair to start falling out. Not much interested in jewelry before she had cancer, Annie started wearing silver bracelets, jeweled earrings, and a necklace with a chunky pendant. Her hairdresser helped her put together a new look. "He told me that bald is a fashion statement."

Eventually science may figure out a cause and a way to prevent the disease and the stalker will slink off, or maybe we'll just burn him at the stake. But in the meantime we worry; we pray to get through this mammogram and that call-back. We promise to love our breasts and not wish they were bigger or smaller or higher. We don't call them boobs or tits. And if it happens to us, we will have many coaches to remind us that we're more than the sum of our pretty parts.

"Live like a lion, completely free of all fear." —a dzogchen tantra

Fifty is the time when most doctors really start leaning on you for the following:

- An annual mammogram to check for breast cancer

- Bone density test to check for osteoporosis or osteopenia, which is an early sign of osteoporosis

- Colonoscopy or sigmoidoscopy and fecal occult blood test to check for colon cancer

- Pap smear to check for cervical cancer

- Cholesterol screening to detect the levels of fat that could lead to heart disease

- Hearing test, because baby boomer ears are particularly vulnerable to hearing loss at an earlier age than their parents were. Remember when you left the Stones concert and your ears were ringing? I SAID, REMEMBER THE TIME . . .

Doctors, Doctors Everywhere

When you hit fifty you begin to understand why there are so many doctors in the yellow pages. Not just the regular kind, but also specialists who suddenly want to look at you—and inside you.

Since Katie Couric already talked about her colonscopy on national TV, let me add an account of my own sigmoidoscopy experience. This check for colon cancer is done while the patient is conscious and involves a long probing device (unlike a colonoscopy, during which you are sedated and have no idea what they're using on you). For me, the worst part of the procedure was when the doctor began a conversation with me, right in the middle of the exam. I was lying on my side trying to will myself into another place and time, at least to the moment when I would be covered up and walking out the door and putting the whole thing literally behind me. But he wanted to chat about something I'd written in the newspaper. He was being friendly, but it was during the part of the examination when we weren't exactly making eye contact, if you know what I mean. I mumbled something like "Yes . . . no . . . let me think about it." I thought about how many physical exams we endure in which we leave our bodies, as if we were dropping off the car for maintenance, allowing the doctor to do what he or she must do in order to keep us healthy. Meanwhile, our real selves wait in the parking lot.

With this in mind, you'll be glad when it's just your feet that need attention.

ONE MORE TIME, THE WARNING SIGNS

We know these. We've read them. We have them taped inside the closet door or medicine cabinet. The earlier you detect breast cancer, the better your chances of surviving. According to the National Cancer Institute, the five-year survival rate for women whose tumors haven't spread beyond the breast is 92 percent. So be a nagging mother to yourself. Do the monthly self-exams, get yearly mammograms, and call the doctor if you notice any of the following changes in your breasts:

- A lump in the breast or under the arm
- A change in the normal size or shape of the breast
- Spontaneous discharge from the nipple
- A change in the color or feel of the skin of the breast or areola
- A sudden onset of pain in the breast

"My [mastectomy] scar is beautiful. It looks like an arrow. . . .
I want to show off my scar proudly and not be afraid of it.
A really strong woman accepts the war she went through
and is ennobled by her scars." —**carly simon**

Take Care of Those Tootsies

There are many annoying things that happen to a body that has been pushed beyond the warranty. This is just one: the foot thing.

It can start out feeling like when you were a kid and your sock crawled down your ankle and bunched up under your foot. Or like you have a pebble in your shoe. But you're in bare feet and getting out of bed and what is going on with that heel?

Most of us take our feet for granted. We may obsess over shoes, but not our feet. When feet realize you care more about some strappy little high-heeled things in pink than about them, they rebel. They even rebel when you put them in what you thought were decent running shoes. You can end up with plantar fasciitis, the leading cause of that pain in the heel that makes you cry, "Ow, ow, ow," all the way from the bedroom to the bathroom.

This condition is so common that when you complain to your doctor she will likely hand you a brochure on plantar fasciitis. You acquire the condition, which is not really the same as heel spurs, through ignorance and abuse. It can come from bad shoes, weight gain, deciding to start training for a marathon without warming up. It can happen to those who run, walk, play tennis, or dance until dawn. The good news is it goes away if you pamper your feet.

Having the condition can also give you license to buy new shoes, although they are more apt to be clogs than stilettos. You become the person in the drugstore staring at the display of gel inserts and heel cups. These will make your feet feel a little better, but they don't work as well as orthotics, fancy inserts you buy in sporting goods stores, or customized ones you special order through your podiatrist and hope your insurance covers.

Plantar fasciitis is one of those conditions that you may never know about until you get it, and then it'll suddenly seem that everyone has it, too. Once you start talking feet problems with people, it sounds like an epidemic. Friends tell you how they bring an ice pack to work for when the pain kicks in, but that a bag of frozen pearl onions will work just as well. They tell you to always keep a golf ball in your purse or by your chair so you can do little roll-around exercises with your foot to give it a workout.

You watch. People will nod their head knowingly when you start to describe the symptoms, and before long they'll be taking off their shoes and showing you their inserts.

Christine Dobrowolski, who wrote the book *Those Aching Feet,* says women often think that it's normal for their feet to hurt. It's not, she promises. But you may have to change your shoes. If you're having problems with your feet, you shouldn't be wearing shoes that let the foot move around very much. That includes flip-flops and ballet flats. Going barefoot is just as bad. High heels are hard on the feet as well, because they tend to put added pressure on the balls of the feet by jamming the foot forward.

Christine's favorite shoe is a clog with a little heel. Her test for a foot-friendly shoe is to try to bend it. Even it's adorable and its color goes smashingly with your best Capri pants, if you can bend it in half it's not going to be your friend. Women who exercise a lot should watch their shoes for wear. Six months is what she gives most shoes used in cross training or serious running. Walking and running shoes can also cause trouble. If they're too lightweight they won't provide support and in three months can start breaking down.

"Shoes take a pounding even on a treadmill," she says. Even if they still look good, if they fold in half like a sandwich, trade them in."

"I remember what Catherine Deneuve always said: 'After a certain age you can have your face or you can have your ass, it's one or the other.' I've chosen my face, and I'll sit on the rest of it ... My laurels, I mean"
—meryl streep

Beautiful Bellies

We know strong abdomens are good for our backs and spines, so we do our push-ups and abdominal curls. Our rectus abdominus and obliques are strong but, oh dear, the belly's still there. Maybe it's telling us we should honor the mature belly.

The round, full stomach is the place from which life springs. It is our little incubator, our all-important center, our hub. As mothers we used it in the way it was intended. During pregnancy, the bigger the belly, the better. Husbands and big brothers, even perfect strangers would touch our bellies and bend over and talk to the creature inside. Then once the baby was out, we started in again complaining about our damn stomachs.

It starts early. We think it's adorable the way little kids walk with their stomachs out for balance. We love those bellies. Then we force those jolly little tummies into designer jeans and the poor kid starts thinking, "I gotta do something about this gut."

No matter how much we women exercise, there will always be an irreducible blip. Ask even a thin one if she dislikes anything about her body, and likely she'll reach down to her belly, grab what she can with two hands, shake it, and say, "Ugh."

We all come from a long line of bellies, but we harbor this need to have a midsection that looks like we don't eat, drink, or sometimes skip the treadmill and read in bed. Our culture has decided that a fleshy belly is a serious flaw. The declaration "That woman has no stomach" is considered a compliment, even though its owner may have binged and purged to get it that way or had it pummeled, stapled, or surgically altered.

Goddess statues have marvelous bellies. Artists have always loved the full-bellied model. I say give the belly a rest. Ditch the belt, free the flesh, unzip, unhook, exhale. Pat it like you love it, for good luck. We need the balance.

Big on Bones

More good news. Bad bones are not a natural part of aging, according to the surgeon general, but the risk of osteoporosis, a disease that weakens the bones and causes them to become porous and brittle, does increase over fifty. It's four times more common in women than in men, and we're more vulnerable after menopause as estrogen levels drop.

There are a number of drugs that claim to treat or prevent osteoporosis, but any woman who remembers the hype and promise of hormone therapy would be wise to use them cautiously and stay current on women's health studies on any drugs.

How Can I Be Having a Heart Attack?

On her way from Salt Lake City to a conference in Seattle, Diane, a school administrator, started feeling dizzy and nauseated. "I told my husband maybe we need to stop and eat," she says. They stopped at the nearest small town and were walking into a restaurant when Diane was suddenly hit by pain across her chest and down her

THINK STRAIGHT & TALL

This is what we need to do:

- Take calcium and vitamin D, because it's D that allows the calcium to get into the bloodstream.

- Do weight-bearing exercises —any activity that works against gravity—such as playing soccer, climbing stairs, walking, weight lifting, and running. They all help to build bones. Exercise also helps increase muscle mass, which helps protect bones from injury.

- Keep the weight off, but not too much. Middle-age spread arrives just in time to protect our bones. Skinny people break easier. Isn't that ironic?

- Stop smoking. Drink in moderation.

- Eat leafy green vegetables, dairy products, and other foods rich in calcium and vitamin D.

KEEP ON TICKING

Cardiovascular disease is the leading cause of death in women and it's mostly preventable by eating right and exercising. Here are some tips from the American Heart Association:

- Do some kind of physical activity for at least thirty minutes every day, even if only for ten minutes at a time.
- Use the stairs instead of the elevator.
- Play with the dog and the grandkids. Don't sit on the bench and watch.
- Schedule physical activity time-outs in your daily planner or computer schedule.
- Take a walk after dinner before slumping in front of the TV.
- Park a few blocks from the office or store and walk.

arm. "I said, 'Something is definitely wrong,' and 'Where is the nearest emergency room?'"

When she got to the hospital she was having a hard time breathing, experiencing symptoms of a heart attack. But Diane, age fifty-one, didn't think she was having a heart attack. The first doctors who looked at her didn't think she was either. But, sure enough, after a number of tests and spending the night in the hospital, an internist decreed, "You've had a heart attack."

"I said, 'How could I have a heart attack? And when? Yesterday, last week?' Apparently I was having one right then in the restaurant and as I walked into the hospital. It was the smartest thing for me to say I'm hungry and we better stop."

From there she was taken by ambulance to Portland, Oregon, four hours away, because it was thought she would need surgery. "I'm like in shock. How could I have had a heart attack and not die? I lay flat in the back of the ambulance and I'm watching all this beautiful scenery, mountains and a big gorge, passing by, my husband following us in our car."

The week before the Seattle conference Diane had gone to see her doctor. "I was so tired. I'd go to work and come home and want to go right to bed, which is unusual for me. I thought I was working too hard. It was the middle of July, very hot in Utah. I felt yucky, nauseated. It was probably preliminary symptoms of a heart attack, but I was blaming my stomach. I had no indications of any heart problems. Never in a million years did I think of myself as [likely to have] a heart attack. I was very healthy, petite. I ate well. I exercised. My cholesterol was good."

In Portland, doctors found no clogged arteries. "They said they didn't know why I had had a heart attack but maybe it was caused by a blood clot. They told me I needed a full workup but I couldn't do it there, and they stabilized me so I could fly back to Salt Lake. My husband was of course scared to death and he had to drive home alone."

While waiting to get an appointment with a cardiologist back home, she had another attack, which felt like the first one but turned out to be more like an aftershock. It was an attack of pericarditis, an inflammation and swelling of the pericardium (the saclike covering of the heart) that can occur in the days or weeks following a heart attack.

That got her into the hospital again in Salt Lake and tests revealed that she had a coronary artery spasm, "a kink in my arteries that had caused the first heart attack. It's a fluky thing that might have been kicked off by stress, a change in altitude from going from sea level to the mountains, any number of reasons that I'll never know."

The next development came when doctors discovered that Diane had a hole in her heart, something she'd apparently been born with and lived with for more than fifty years.

- Get up from your desk or computer and walk around.
- Hide the remote control and change TV channels the old-fashioned way.
- Concentrate on foods that reduce high blood cholesterol, high blood pressure, and excess weight, the major risk factors for heart attack and stroke.
- Eat fruits, vegetables, beans, nuts, fish, poultry, lean meats, cereal and grain products, and fat-free and low-fat dairy products.
- Try water with a slice of lemon or lime instead of soda.
- Eat with others. You'll eat slower and less.
- Keep a healthy snack stash (such as carrots, nuts, and celery) so you won't hit the candy machine when you get the munchies.

Diane's practiced at telling her story and yet she still seems amazed at its twists and turns and the irony of it all. "When they told me I had a hole in my heart I thought back and said, no wonder I couldn't do track. I've always been running on half fuel." Surgery repaired the hole so that Diane can say, "Now my heart is very, very good. You can't even tell I had a heart attack. I am very well, heartwise."

But the story doesn't end there. The pericarditis requires that she stay on prednisone, which has caused her to gain weight. Now thirty pounds over her normal weight, she's jumped from a size four to a size ten. "I'm not used to this new person. I feel kind of blocklike, although everyone thinks I look good for what I've gone through."

One more thing. There was a brain tumor, discovered during a routine MRI, which was part of her follow-up heart care. It was benign and it was removed before it caused any bad effects. Otherwise it might have grown, doctors said, and eventually impacted her vision.

She laughs and says, "Can you believe it? I thought things like this didn't happen until your seventies and eighties." However, with both head and heart now fixed, Diane says, "I'm very grateful to be alive and have another chance to get on with my life. I feel like there's been chapter one and chapter two. Chapter one is before. I was very active, outgoing, a workaholic. Now I'm in chapter two, trying to find a balance. I'm not as aggressive as I used to be. I won't be the top-notch administrator I anticipated being in this time of my life but it's a good thing. I'm only working part-time and in the job and my home life I try to not have to do it all. I'm learning to delegate."

Diane's second job is helping to educate other women about heart disease. "I spread the word. I go to seminars. I do the heart walks. I go on TV. Women still don't know enough about it. They still think it's a man's problem. I tell women to pay attention to diet. I tell them to be aware of pain in the jaw, the neck area, the back. I tell them not to get overtired. I don't think women realize how young you can be and have a heart attack."

For her fiftieth birthday, before the heart attack, Diane and her husband went to Key West for a blowout celebration. "I was looking forward to my fifties. I've never been afraid of aging. Turning fifty was the best time in my life. Then this happened. That's another thing I tell women. Celebrate what you have right now."

WE HAVE DIFFERENT SYMPTOMS

It wasn't until the early 1990s that medicine began separating men's and women's versions of heart disease. Traditionally women were considered to be like little men with the same responses to heart problems. But there can be big differences. Some women, like Diane, have symptoms weeks before a heart attack. Women also have unexplained fatigue before their heart attacks, while men often go to see their doctors with chest pain. Some of the other differences include the following:

- Women feel discomfort or pain in the upper body or chest lasting more than a few minutes. Men have a tightening and pressure in the chest or arms and discomfort in the neck or upper back, often between the shoulder blades.
- Women's pain moves to the shoulder, neck, arms, jaw, teeth, or back and spreads around. Men often feel a sharp, burning or cramping pain.
- Women can experience a sudden weakness. Men have a generalized weakness.
- Women complain of unusual tiredness. Men have severe fatigue and anxiety.
- Women feel light-headed. Men become pale.
- Women often feel a loss of appetite. Men have a feeling of fullness.

My Menopause, Myself

We should have known there would be no miracle way to get through menopause. To count on one perfect pill to work for all menopausal women was as foolish as trusting a one-size-fits-all dress to look any better than a muumuu. Yet we'd hoped that once we started to have symptoms we could take a tab of estrogen and another of progesterone and we would be strong of heart and clear of mind forever. We would also have creamy skin, thick hair (on our heads, not our chins), and multiple orgasms forever. And, of course, because boomers believe that the clock should stop for us, we wanted something to make us look and feel like we were not getting older.

That's what the pharmaceutical companies and our doctors told us and what we wanted to believe. And so, millions of us held out our hands, stuck out our tongues, shut up, and took our pills.

We were duped. In 2002 the Women's Health Initiative, the government-funded health study on the risks and benefits of hormone replacement therapy (HRT), showed that the standard hormone cocktail that women had been taking for decades was actually putting us at higher risk for the very things we had taken them to avoid. The news caused a stunning reversal; the annual use of HRT dropped from 18.5 million to 7.6 million women between 2002 and 2004, according to the American Medical Association.

We weaned; we tapered. Some went cold turkey. I was in Colorado my first week off hormones and I'll never be sure if my need to sit in a bathtub with the lights off rather than hike those gorgeous mountains had to do with altitude sickness or hormone deprivation. In retrospect, it was pretty amazing that millions of women going off a drug they had trusted to keep them sane and healthy did not commit multiple acts of violence. Yet there were no swarms of betrayed consumers storming the headquarters of the major pill pushers. No reports of large numbers of middle-aged women wandering mall parking lots unable to find their cars.

But menopause continues to be a fact of life, and somewhere between the ages of forty and fifty-eight we still must deal with it, not as a disease, but as an unavoidable physical and psychological transition. The best thing that came out of the hormone conundrum was that women decided we each have to figure out what's best for ourselves. Some women, after dropping hormones, went back on them. Doctors said that for some women HRT is the only way to get symptom relief, but they could become dangerous after more than five years. So drugmakers came out with low-dose versions of their old brands. Some women switched to "natural" or "bio-identical" hormones, which are said to be identical in molecular composition to those the body makes, although some experts maintain that customized hormones are no safer than synthetic.

Like women have learned to do with other shared events, such as childbirth, we tap all sources for advice and recommendations—doctors, books, medical Web sites—and then we talk to our sympathetic allies. Their stories vary. Susan works in a pharmacy and said when she was younger she noticed that the patients who picked up their hormone pills every month looked better than the ones who did not. She mentioned this to a colleague, who said the difference might be more about lifestyle than pills since the same women looked pretty fit. Maybe they just went to the gym a lot and ate right and that, as much as the pills, made a big difference. Years later, when Susan went into menopause she automatically opted for hormone supplements. But they made her miserable. Her breasts hurt, and she gained weight. "It felt like early pregnancy without the good part." She decided to try the other route. She began exercising, boosted her calcium, and lost weight. Now in her mid-fifties and through menopause, Susan declares she's never felt or looked better in her life. She adds that her mother never took hormones and swims daily at the age of eighty-five—so maybe Susan's lucked out on genes.

Then there's Phyllis, who used to say she would willingly continue to have monthly periods for the rest of her life if she could feel like she did before starting menopause. "I had a flat feeling, an I-could-care-less feeling," says Phyllis. "I had that look in my eyes that certain women get around menopause. That scared, angry look."

Phyllis didn't want to do the traditional hormone combo because she didn't trust it. "It felt like I was taking poison." She went to a gynecologist who created a customized dose of natural hormones, referred Phyllis to an herbalist, and recommended that she start working out.

Phyllis said she feels like "a new version of my old self," partly because of the natural hormones, which she only took for less than a year, but also because she got into tap dancing and race walking. To temper hot flashes, she avoids drinking wine and sleeping under flannel sheets.

In between the experiences of Susan and Phyllis are those of millions of women doing menopause in their own way. Some will need no help getting through it. Some who have done everything the natural way their whole lives and plan to do the same with menopause will be stunned by how their body turns on them overnight. The most troubling symptoms are the same as they've always been—hot flashes, decreased libido, insomnia, and mood swings.

But the ways of handling them will likely continue to expand from traditional to nontraditional. And with a dose of humor, in the way of cartoonist Dee Adams who strives to teach that menopause isn't fatal in her "Minnie Pauz" characters.

There are reasons that women initially called their hormone supplements everything from "my pretty pill" to "my real self pill." We thought they were our friend. But there are alternatives. The woman who doesn't want to take hormones because of the cancer risk but has an alarmingly low libido may need something for vaginal dryness. Or a weekend away with a patient lover. The woman who feels mentally off and anxious may do better on a short course of antidepressants than hormones. But no woman should do anything without lots of research and talking to a doctor she trusts.

Of course, hormones still have their loyal fans. I know a woman who has been taking hormones for three decades, and when I asked her why, she patted her nearly unlined eighty-four-year-old cheeks.

Menopause is a big marker. The body sweats. The mind freezes. There is often serious thought to changing your name and running off to South America. But there is also something that is real and exciting and is often referred to as "post-menopausal zest." You know the older friend who runs circles around you like a puppy? She got through menopause. So will we all. Menopause is often called "the change." But not "the end."

COOLING THE FLASH

The most annoying and telling symptom of menopause is a hot flash. You sweat and you haven't even moved. You blush and it's not becoming. Your body is on fire, but you're not at all turned on. It's not fun. However, there are ways to cope without taking powerful drugs. These hints come from the National Women's Health Network and some long-time flashers.

- Avoid or cut back on coffee, chocolate, spicy foods, and alcohol, which can aggravate hot flashes.
- Dress in layers. Be prepared to shed clothes without embarrassing yourself.
- Be wary of turtlenecks and anything close to the skin that is remotely like wool. Wear a cotton or silk tank underneath.
- Sleep in the nude or under light blankets to temper night sweats. Don't tuck in the covers.
- Fans work. Placing battery-operated ones in your office may mark you as menopausal, but don't be surprised if the other women in the building start stopping by to chat. Paper fans are fun and you can match them with your outfit or just go with a red one.
- Breathe. Slow, deep breathing helps control a hot flash.
- Herbs can be helpful, but they're tricky. What helps one woman can cause hives in the next. Talk to an herbalist, read the latest information, and experiment with caution.
- Seek out a cooling environment. Take long walks on a foggy beach.

Hair Wars

Maybe if we could come up with a jazzier word for gray we'd like it better. Something that didn't sound so dull and ordinary. We could borrow ideas from the paint-chip people. Call it "flint" or "ice" or "morning fog." As in, "Jean, who has a flint-colored bob and seawater green eyes . . ." Or, "Her hair, a swirl of morning fog, made his heart go pitty-pat."

But so far, we seem to be pretty much stuck with gray, both in our hair follicles and our image of it. Gray is the big age marker. No denying it. No one is prepared for it. All gray hair is premature when it shows up on your head. Keeping your gray can also be a mark of maturity and elegance and simple defiance. But it's a bold act and that's probably why we talk about it so much.

Kate has had shiny silver hair since her early forties. It was part of her signature. She was defiantly gray, then white, while all of her father's wives had dyed their hair. She decided she would stay natural. But in her late fifties she started weakening and added some golden brown streaks. "It's easier to have gray hair when you're younger," she says, adding that at her last conference she counted only two naturally graying heads, even though she knows the participants to be decidedly middle aged.

What to do with our hair is a common struggle. It has nothing to do with world peace, which is probably why you're more likely to see *People* magazine than *Atlantic Monthly* at the hair salon. But I bet even Mother Teresa had her bad hair days. At least she always had a scarf handy.

"Gray hair just doesn't look good on me," says Miriam. "It looks good on some women but it makes me feel old. It's easier to do something about than brown spots, which I hate even more. Hair is one of the few things we can control. We can go to the drugstore and buy an $8 box of hair dye. You can't buy something to become taller or change your eye color."

And why wouldn't we still be fussing about our hair at fifty, says Miriam, considering we've had a lifetime of it. "When you're a little girl people start messing with your hair. They don't do that with little boys. But with girls they're always doing something, putting it in pigtails, clipping it in barrettes. They did it when I was little and they're still doing it with little girls today. You have a one-year-old who hasn't any hair at all, and someone sticks a bow on her head."

Joanie started going gray in her late thirties, and "not in a good way, in little tufts. I'd rather not have to do something and if I had nice gray hair like my husband's maybe I wouldn't," she says. She dyes her hair dark brown with a reddish tinge, which is close to her natural color. "If I was really into it, I'd make it browner during the winter and redder in the summer. But I don't want to go that far."

Coloring your hair is an expensive, messy, and time-consuming habit. But it's safer, less expensive, and more reversible than getting your nose reshaped or those smile lines erased. "On most women gray hair takes away something," says Miriam. "Even on the strong, beautiful ones, it changes them. It's not right, and I hate that I think that way, but I don't see it changing in my lifetime," says Miriam. For her, hair worries go back to childhood. "Remember Barbie's friend Skipper? She had long auburn hair. I was so jealous of her hair I would throw her in the pool just to mess it up."

Cait says she dyes her white hair blonde every time she changes jobs, twice now in her fifties. "People look at your gray hair and they close down." On the other hand, Charlotte, an actress in Detroit, dyed her hair until she was fifty. She now says, "These wrinkles and gray hair have gotten me more parts than my acting skills."

I suppose you could take a vow after some age that it's not worth the effort and maybe not politically correct to dye one's hair, but then you'd run into a woman you know to be your age with a brand-new gold-streaked, tousled Jane Fonda hairdo. And you'd think, why not? One thing about gray is that it always comes back.

Never Too Late for a 2:00 A.M. Feeding

A fifty-six-year-old woman had twins in 2004 and was proclaimed the oldest mother of twins on record, but then someone else came up with a fifty-seven-year-old mother of twins, and soon after that a fifty-nine-year-old in Georgia alerted the media that she too had twins on the way. You read about a woman having a baby past fifty and you automatically get lower back pain and start doing the math.

What you come up with is that these women will be deep into their sixties when their kids become teenage aliens, and in their seventies at their kids' weddings. Good grief—in their eighties they may be lending their own granny apartment to their boomerang kid who's moved back home to find himself.

Hearing about even a single birth at this age causes shivers among those who consider the fifties a time to start emptying the nest, not building a new wing onto it. But there are no term limits on maternal urges. Nor, apparently, on what modern medicine can provide. Middle-aged mommies are on the rise. In 2003 there were more than fifteen hundred first-time mothers between the ages of forty-five and fifty-four, according to the Centers for Disease Control and Prevention.

Lucy, a college instructor and therapist, had her first baby at age thirty-seven, and her second at fifty-four. She and I talked soon after her sixtieth birthday party and her daughter's fifth. When Lucy married her husband, who also had a son from a previous marriage, she decided she wasn't through having babies. Even though she was over fifty she longed for another child and hoped for a daughter. And she got one.

The experience has proved magical and exhausting. "It's better than the best I imagined and some parts were worse than the worst I imagined. The better wins. I've got my daughter. All through my forties I tried to substitute for having more children. I collected animal pets, dolls, took on more female clients, added more students. But none of these helped. I had daughter dreams every week. Finally my new husband agreed that we could try to have a child, our only child together. We have been so lucky to have Madeline.

Lucy says the plus in being an older mom is that she's more relaxed than she was the first time around. Both she and her husband feel they have more confidence and wisdom than they did as first-time parents twenty years before, "even though our sons have come out quite whole."

Lucy makes jokes about her situation, but they're based on the reality that sometimes this older mom feels a bit like an outsider. "I differed with some of the younger women at the preschool, over how late to use the bottle. My attitude is as long as they're not drinking from the bottle in kindergarten, they'll be okay. I'm in so many different worlds. I'm with twenty- and thirty-year-old mothers at the preschool and then I'm swimming at the pool on my senior discount. Nobody quite believes me at either place." Some of her daughter's friends want to know if Lucy is her grandmother. Adults are usually more tactful. "They inquire in a roundabout way, asking, 'Who is this child to you?'"

It did give Lucy pause when her daughter asked if her mother would die before she grew up. "We had a little talk. I told her that women in our family tend to live a long time, my grandma to age ninety-nine. I told her that she has her father and older brothers and there are others who can act like mommies even if your mommy dies."

For her, staying fit and healthy is an imperative. And so, to a degree, is looking younger. "In my fifties I let my hair grow white, but now I feel I have to dye it brown to look younger. I also try to keep my weight down to look younger. I try to avoid getting sick, which sometimes happens more often at my age. Staying healthy goes into deciding how much I work, sleep, things I didn't worry so much about before.

Lucy's daughter has also inspired a new career direction for her. She's considering leaving her practice and stopping teaching in order to concentrate on writing, after having her first poem published in a literary magazine and beginning a four-generation memoir.

"It's a cliché that having a child keeps you young. The truth of it is you don't have a choice. There are days I long to sit in the sun in a chair by myself and not have three things going on at once. On the other hand I have tremendous energy. I take vitamins, go to the gym, exercise an hour a day, swim three days a week. My body's older but my heart's much younger. Nothing is more enchanting than our five-year-old daughter singing grace as we sit down to dinner."

Miriam had her child at thirty-nine and said she always identified with actress Anne Bancroft, who did the same. "I always read whatever she had to say about being a mother and if she ever felt like she missed out on anything. I'm always reading about older mothers. To see how old they are now and how much time they might have with their children as adults. I worry about the time I didn't get by waiting to have kids."

On the other hand, she sees the advantages. "I know people who went from college to marriage to having kids. While they were having kids I was working. Now, after fifty, when I look for another job I don't feel as desperate as someone might who hasn't been in the work world. I know how to interview. I know how the business world works."

Like Lucy, Miriam's determined to be a fit and healthy mother to her child at any age. "I can keep up physically with my son as an older mother. I probably won't take him waterskiing, but I probably wouldn't have done that if I'd had him at twenty-five."

"Look, my feet hurt some mornings and my body is less forgiving when I exercise more than I'm used to. But I love my life more, and me more. I'm so much juicier. And like that old saying goes, it's not that I think less of myself, but that I think of myself less often. And that feels like heaven to me." **—anne lamott**

When the Wee Birds Fly Away

Cartoonist Lynn Johnston, creator of *For Better or for Worse,* said that when she wanted another baby she added a little girl to her comic strip family. That's one way to deal with an empty nest, but not everyone has the imagination or opportunity to mentally fill that back bedroom when the last kid moves out.

"At first I had to keep telling myself, they're not dead; they're just at college," says Kat, in Boston. "A wise friend who has raised four kids poured me a rum and grapefruit juice drink and hugged me and every time I started sniffling would say, 'Yes, this is exactly how you are supposed to be feeling.' I ate a lot of oatmeal raisin cookies and other comfort foods those first few weeks and thought—briefly—about adopting another child or maybe a third dog."

In an essay about the empty nest syndrome for More.com, writer Sara Peyton wrote, "What I really miss when there are no kids around is the delicious feeling that my day-to-day decisions, large and small—how I spent my time, what I cooked for supper, why I made money, and why it was never enough—confirmed my place in the world and made me feel I was on the right path. On days when I felt angry or depressed the bonds to my kids reassuringly tethered me to my husband, my home, my community, my work, the very ground I walked on, and even the vegetables I grew in my garden."

With her kids now in graduate school she has put her energy into in-line skating, kayaking, skiing, and buying a new bicycle, "the first one that wasn't a hand-me-down from my kids." And there's a new black standard poodle in the house—not the kind of dog that would appeal to a man or her two boys, but it's definitely Sara's and "follows me around like my toddlers once did."

Pets help fill an empty nest. If you adopt a dog, the puppy period itself will make you happy you are no longer having babies. Or get a horse. They take up even more time and eat almost as much as a teenager. Here are some other ways to deal with the melancholy that goes along with an empty nest:

- Visit a friend whose teenagers are still home, particularly the kind who mumble, think all adults are annoying, and constantly say, *Why isn't there anything to eat in this house?*

- Enjoy the new closet space. Fill it as soon as possible with your things. Box up all of the kids' stuff and move it to the garage, where it will stay until you finally put the house on the market and have a garage sale.

- Take up contra dancing or something else that will surprise even your kids.

- If you really miss having a kid around, volunteer at a school. Become a soccer coach. Mentor. Become a court appointed special advocate (CASA) through a program that pairs adults with kids who are under the protection of the court system.

Mama's Got a New Pair of Dancing Shoes

When Leslie's last child left home for college she volunteered to work weekends at her friend's pumpkin farm. "I thought I would completely fall apart that first month, so I made a commitment to help a friend who lived out of town. I was really terrified of coming home on a Friday afternoon from work and the house being empty. I was away for five weekends, and by the time I came home I was happy to be there."

Leslie raised three sons pretty much as a single mother and made it her life for twenty-three years, without much grousing. "I was totally committed to being with them. I enjoyed it.

They're great kids, fun to hang out with. At one point in my motherhood I read something that Jacqueline Kennedy said, that no matter what you do in your life, it doesn't mean a thing if you didn't raise your kids well. It stuck in my head."

For several years she home-schooled them until it became impossible to do that and also work at her sales job. She went back to college and started teaching elementary school, which offered better hours and a more secure income. But beginning teachers don't make much and so she worked weekends at a hospital job and summers at the county fair. "I really didn't do much else but work and be with my kids." And then they started to leave. Leslie keeps a Mother's Day card on her mantel that one of her sons made. "It's a picture of a nest and the birds are out and flying around."

At least it's now a clean nest. "The biggest bonus was not having to do so much housework and cooking. I wasn't a fast-food mom. I was in the grocery store every other day, cooking for them and their friends. I now clean every two weeks and go to the grocery store only once a week."

Then Leslie threw herself into contra dancing, a form of square dancing with live music in which dancers switch partners and make lots of eye contact. "It's very flirtatious, in a safe way," says Leslie, who can tell you just about every venue in the San Francisco Bay Area that has a contra night.

"A few years ago a friend told me to try contra dancing, that it was a good way to meet men. At first I was shy. I'd go with a girlfriend and I wouldn't talk to anyone and hide during the breaks. Sometimes I'd sit out dances because I was too afraid to ask someone to dance."

But now she's out dancing sometimes three nights a week, even after teaching grade school all day. "I think my mentality changed once my last son left and I got more assertive. I've gotten into the flare of dancing. You can be totally outrageous with no worry of sending out the wrong message. I do all this fancy moving around. I think I'm feeling truly single now, and I'm not going to sit out any more dances."

In her early fifties, she's also figuring out her next career step. She might take a teaching job in another country, rent out her California house, and take a leave from her current job. In preparation she's taken a course in teaching English as a second language and is getting a Spanish language teaching credential.

"I have options now, but I have to plan. Maybe I'll find a way to retire in Mexico."

Mom and Dad Are Doing It

The big news about sex after fifty is that it's not uncommon and it continues. Sex guru Sue Johanson, of Canada, came up with a word for older women who enjoy sex and intend to have it as long as they're able. She calls them "cougars"—a description that conjures a hungry, muscular, animal image, far better than thinking of yourself as shut down for life.

It's a silly prejudice to think that sex belongs to young people. Why should they get all the good stuff? Actually we're more practiced at sex. We've tried a few variations and we know what we like. We're not afraid to ask for it. We can't get pregnant. And we have learned to be patient.

A study by AARP reported the pleasant findings that midlife and older people enjoy sex, find it essential in their lives, and don't want to give it up. As well, one-third reported that they have sex at least once a week. And since their last report, AARP found that oral sex is up and so is self-stimulation.

So there.

Neva's son regularly sends his parents new music, "in an effort to keep us current, but he also likes to send us 'get it on' music just for the two of us. My mother would die at the thought."

Music is a regular part of their romantic evenings. "On really steamy nights we like sliding over one another like chocolate to Miles Davis, Al Green, Norah Jones," says Neva. "When we heard Van Morrison in concert we came home and put his music on, and after going to the symphony, Rachmaninoff worked for us. I like to light candles, set up the music, open the windows. Maybe put on something exotic or flowing or just a short T-shirt."

Stacy, a doctor, says that if there is a fountain of youth, it's sex. "When I'm having sex I feel like a twenty-year-old." Then she thinks a minute. "That really depends on who I'm with. Sometimes I feel like a forty-two-year-old."

In many ways the need goes beyond sex. "On a rainy night I want someone who is also my friend, the witness to my life," says Stacy.

Elvira is one of the writers with the Kensington Ladies' Erotica Society, a group that has authored three books starting with the then-shocking *Ladies' Own Erotica* in 1980. Having spent more than twenty-five years talking about their favorite subject with readers across the country, the "Ladies" report mixed reviews of Viagra. Elvira says she personally finds Viagra "a little coercive. No matter what we say to men about what we want in lovemaking, they want the power hit they get from having a hard hard-on. I think many older women are happy with a more laid-back sex life. Slow and romantic, please. How loud do we have to scream that?"

Some women are apparently quite adept at making their desires known. If you have the right partner and the right attitude, author Joan Price says sex can become "fabulous in ways we never expected." In interviewing older women for her book *Better Than I Ever Expected: Straight Talk About Sex After 60,* Joan found that yes, the sex drive does recede, "as far as the gotta-have-it-right-now feelings of urgency and the physical drive itself. And our genital tissues thin, we lose lubrication, and, to some extent, sensitivity. Our bodies and our minds need much more warm-up than they used to.

"But that's the good news as well, because leisurely sex with lots of touching and laughing is great sex. For the first time, we're more evenly matched to our partners, if our partners are

This is what I know about sex after a certain age:

- It's good for your complexion and your heart and it burns calories.

- It almost always makes you like him better in the morning.

- Your friends always sound like they're having more sex than you are, but they may be thinking the same of you.

- You always run into someone you recognize at a sex shop.

- In studies men report greater dissatisfaction with their sex lives, but women bitch about it much more to their friends.

- The sex is a gentler romp, more slow hand. The pillows stay at the head of the bed or under a sore hip instead of being flung to the floor.

- You never lose your taste for deep kissing. Or for spooning.

- Blessed be lubricants.

our age, because they also need more warm-up," says Joan. "There's nothing better than two people who come to each other in love, with a whole lot of life experience behind them, and who know their own bodies and can communicate. That's why I say I'm having the best sex of my life, at age sixty-one, and most of the women I interviewed said the same thing. We may be having sex less often, and we may not feel ocean waves crashing quite as hard, but, wow, rocking gently on those waves for a good hour until they build high enough to take us over—it doesn't get much better than that."

Wife of Grumpy

Psychotherapist Jed Diamond wrote about grumpy men like himself in *The Irritable Male Syndrome* following his best-selling book *Male Menopause*. It's probably no surprise that more women bought his books than men. Wives and girlfriends were eager to figure out why their men were so out of sorts and they were also relieved to discover they weren't the only women who wished they'd ended up with Mr. Congeniality instead of Mr. Edgy.

The author wrote *Male Menopause* when he was entering his fifties, a dangerous time for men in relation to self-esteem. He admits he wasn't pleasant to be around, but he sought help and wrote a book about it. In his late fifties he decided to study anger and depression in men and concluded that men's depression is expressed through irritability, hence *The Irritable Male Syndrome.*

In the meantime his wife, Carlin Diamond, was going through her own menopause. Fortunately, she, too, is a therapist and ended up becoming an expert in how to stay married to a grumpy man.

The Irritable Male Syndrome is caused, according to Jed Diamond's studies, by hormonal fluctuations, biochemical changes, threats to masculine identity, and increased stress. The classic irritable male comes across as angry, impatient, blaming, dissatisfied, moody, fearful, discontented, hypersensitive, exhausted, and grumpy. Carlin Diamond says she's met very few women who don't "get" the meaning of the syndrome.

When Jed Diamond was going through his irritable period Carlin decided that if he didn't get a grip in two years she'd leave the marriage. "I found I was going along with his moods, just drifting. There came a time when I realized we were drifting into a stagnant pond. It's a trap that women get into. We accommodate. We're flexible. But after a while, a kind of coldness comes into your insides. You start to shut down."

Giving herself two years to see if they could mend things, she says, "was such a relief. It gave me time to get back on my feet. To work out our stuff, his and mine. We made it through."

Carlin sees a similar resolve in her women friends and clients to confront rather than acquiesce. "Huge changes happen when women hit menopause. They go from being the woman who needs the man for emotional support to making a huge unconscious shift. We don't have that binding need for a man and a nest and a family. The kids are gone and you reevaluate the old guy. We get pickier.

"I really see women raising their heads. We're healthier in our older age now. We're financially independent. We hit fifty and realize we have thirty to forty years of good productive life left and do we really want to continue picking up after this guy and being miserable? Our mother's generation kind of gave up at that age. Oh well, they thought. This is better than being on my own. Women today don't necessarily feel that way."

You might expect that two therapists, especially people who counsel other couples, would have a model relationship. Not so, says Carlin. "When it's your own personal stuff, you do a lot of dodges. You'd rather have external harmony and avoid going to that deep painful point. You think, 'Oh, well, he's just in a bad mood.' But after saying 'Oh, well' two thousand times you realize you need to stop and talk about it."

She's believes that's the only thing that works—talking about the really painful issues. "For us that's been the glue, to face our pain, no matter what it is. Face it down until there's some resolve. It's almost like a birth pain, but each time our relationship would broaden and deepen to some kind of spiritual understanding. The result can be so positive, and the next time it happens you remember that you can get through this. You want aliveness in the relationship, and there's not aliveness if you put things on the back burner."

How to Stay Married for Forty Years

Terry shares one of those private moments between couples. One morning, as she and her husband, Lyman, stood naked together in front of the mirror after a shower, she said, "I started to laugh and said, 'Look at us. If you met me in a singles bar today would you ask me out?' And he said, 'Of course I would.'"

This is a man who's obviously practiced at giving the right answer. But Terry says that from the beginning he knew how to charm her. A girlfriend of Terry's introduced them, after Terry had fled her first husband and taken her son to another state. Lyman let her know that he considered this gorgeous young woman and her young son to be a package deal. "For our first date he asked if he could take me and Jimmy to the zoo." Of course she fell in love with him. It also helped, she said, that "he was just out of the Army and beautiful and he had a brand-new red sports car. I was lusting for him immediately."

Six weeks later he asked her to marry him. They recently celebrated their fortieth anniversary over chocolate martinis. They have four children, Terry's first child, whom Lyman adopted, two more adopted kids, and a child they had together. It's not all been merry, of course. They've had family troubles, most of which they keep private, and Lyman's been seriously ill twice. "Sometimes I think our life is a Woody Allen movie."

But, she says, "I always have felt adored by him. My girlfriends say I don't deserve him. They say he's the most perfect person and I'm a bitch. One of my friends jokes and introduces him as her future husband."

And sex? "Let's face it—after forty years of marriage that unbridled lust you experienced most of your waking hours during the first few years is going to wane. But if you're one of the lucky ones, it can be replaced with a far deeper intimacy and emotional connection between two people. They say the best thing parents can do for their children is to love one another and I'd like to think we are good role models for ours. Holding hands, finding my coffee made for me when I get up, 'I love you' e-mails during the day help keep the spark alive."

That, and perhaps the fact that they've slept in the nude every night since they got married. "When I got home from a recent trip to Oklahoma, Lyman picked me up at the airport and the first thing I saw on the table were red gladiolas, a bottle of wine, and a $50 bill. 'What's that for?' I asked. He grinned and said, 'A night of wild sex?'"

But really tough stuff can happen when two people are together for a long time. After having a pacemaker implanted for heart problems, Lyman was hit twice by cancer. "A real bad gene pool, as they say," says Terry, trying to laugh. "It's changed our relationship, facing it together. It's allowed us to be far more open and honest, facing for the first time that we're on Earth for a very short time and you'd better say what you have to say while you can."

At first she was in denial. "He would try to talk about wanting to make sure that I'll be okay when he's not around and I would change the subject." Finally her longtime friend told Terry that she was making it worse by not listening to his concerns. So, they became a team. "Some mornings I say we're taking a day off tomorrow from cancer, and we go to lunch or to the casino."

LIKE IS A MANY SPLENDORED THING

If you're going to make it for the long haul, you'd better like the person as well as be madly in love with him.

Here are some hints from the world of the happily married:

- **From a teacher married to a plumber:** Keep laughing. A shared sense of absurdity will get you through many rough spots.

- **From a realtor married to a social worker:** Work with your differences. You're really good at finances and he shouldn't be around a checkbook. He has great mechanical abilities, so he gets to be in charge of the tools.

- **From two married union leaders:** Pick your fights. Winning sometimes matters more to one than to the other. Okay, he's right: he *is* superior at loading the dishwasher. But if it's a matter of huge importance, like whether to move to a condo in Tucson, stand your ground.

- **From an ex-nun married to an ex-priest:** Life is short. Enjoy each other. Leave poems under pillows.

- **From two married writers:** Be willing to make up. Mature people know when it's appropriate to say, "I was being a jerk. Wanna catch a movie?" Depending on the enormity of the offense, "I'm sorry" usually works. "Sorry, sorry, sorry" is better.

- **From a craftswoman married to a craftsman:** Sex keeps things lively and takes the edge off. After making love you're not so quick to find fault with the little annoying things, like wet towels left on the floor.

- **From a librarian married to a photographer:** When all else fails, get counseling. Sometimes you need a reminder from an outside source that one person cannot be all things to the other.

- **From an actress married to a truck driver:** Give each other his or her own time. "If I didn't have my own time I wouldn't be able to act, but when I'm gone he gets out his guitar and plays and does his things."

- **From a sales rep married to a student:** Accept peculiarities. Recognize that his snoring, while maddening, may be only slightly more annoying than your teeth grinding.

- **From a lawyer married to an editor:** Negotiate. You'll have his glass-blowing class over for dinner if he'll go to your niece's wedding and dance.

- **From an author married to a teacher:** Go for separate and equal. Separate work phones, separate e-mail addresses. Sometimes separate bank accounts. Maintain separate offices or getaway spots in the house, with separate computers. If you work at opposite ends of the house you can send each other messages like "Hot tub at six. I have champagne."

Now let's talk about separate vacations.

Guilt Trip for the Perfect Couple

Longstanding couples come to realize that traveling together is delightful, but the occasional separate vacation is also healthy for the relationship. Before you wave good-bye, however, you both need to understand the concept of guilt credits. Guilt credits are what the person who stays at home earns when the other goes away. At some point, the away person will feel sorry that he or she has left behind the beloved to feed the animals and water the garden. The at-home person knows this and banks on this sentiment to rationalize his or her own future getaway. If the balance is maintained, neither person needs to ever feel guilty or abandoned, since you both know there is payback coming. Let's say one person goes off to Phoenix with his buddies to ride motorcycles for two weeks. The at-home person can reasonably figure she has two weeks coming, or at least three long weekends, to spend with her daughters in New York or girlfriends in Chicago, as she chooses.

For this system to work the couple needs to acknowledge that while they love each other madly they don't always thrill to the same things. As a successful couple you need to agree on the big things, like how to raise children and whether to live in the city or the suburbs. That accomplished, you can agree to disagree on what sounds like fun on a long weekend—visiting Civil War burial grounds or going to tai chi camp.

Still There for Her

Vivienne got her bachelor's degree at age sixty-three. At the commencement ceremony she wore summa cum laude colors, and a photo of her late husband, Hutch, tucked inside her bra. She wanted him to be with her as she walked up to the podium and accepted her degree in art history.

They were married for ten years but had known each other for more than thirty, first meeting when they worked together in Auckland, New Zealand. When they finally married, Vivienne was forty-nine and Hutch was eighty. The age difference didn't alarm Vivienne or her friends. He looked the perfect dashing older man and she the ideal adoring younger woman. In truth they were equal partners.

"I'd had romances, but friends always said it would take a special guy to marry me. Hutch was that special guy. I'd known him for twenty years. We'd been friends, no romance, but I knew the quality of this man. A friend who knew us both told me, 'Even if you have only four years you'll have four great years.'" They married the year after his first wife died, and Vivienne moved with him to California.

With his background in the Foreign Service and international journalism, he could tell stories about working for George Patton and being stationed in Paris under the Marshall Plan. He was a sophisticated, cosmopolitan man who wrote for wine magazines and taught Vivienne how to cook.

He convinced her to go to college in her fifties. "He always knew I felt lacking in education," says Vivienne, who had dropped out of high school but worked her way up from a clerk's position to director of the United States Information Services in Auckland.

He was ill only part of his last year of life, but, looking back, Vivienne can see now that he had prepared for the eventuality. "I remember him insisting we sell a perfectly good car for a new one, saying I wouldn't have to worry about another car for seven years." And he convinced her to become an American citizen so she'd have no difficulty receiving his government benefits.

He left her in good shape financially and with the goal of finishing her degree. Vivienne says he also motivated her to go on and be as vigorous and active as he was until right before he died at eighty-nine. The year after he died she signed up for a group hike in Tuscany and prepared by taking an intensive Italian language course.

"I made up my mind that I am not going to just fade away. I'd rather be traveling with Hutch. We always had so much fun together. But I'm a single person now and it is up to me to be outgoing and do things. I imagine him saying, 'Of course you can do it.'"

"Arrange whatever pieces come your way." **—virginia woolf**

A Death in Paris

When Erika met film director Robert Kramer she had just come from an ashram in Sri Lanka and he from North Vietnam, where he'd filmed American bombings of the country in 1969. "The yin-yang combustion was volatile and fertile," says Erika. "Robert, a martial artist, and me, a dancer, yoga life artist. We were a polarity love dance. In French they say 'un couple passionel.'"

Thirty years later, after an international life filled with creativity, love, and politics, Robert died in Paris at age sixty, of meningitis. By then he had become well known, more in Europe than the United States, as an avant-garde and experimental filmmaker, and he and Erika had put down new roots in France. When he was dying Erika connected with friends and fans around the world to hold an electronic vigil and prayer circle.

After he died, California-born Erika remained in France. More European than American in style at least, today she bicycles through the city streets, her hair in long silver braids, continuing to do body-healing work for clients in her Paris studio. On a recent June evening she wrote from Paris, "The summer night gray light lingers until almost eleven o'clock. It's my birthday week. My heart has begun to celebrate life in harmony with the occasion. Today I had a long talk with a friend on the phone who just spent a month with his mom until she died of an explosive cancer. We talked about the gift of death, the grace of sharing death with someone you love. Since becoming a widow, there has been a stream of deaths and partners of death flowing through my life. It's as if Robert prepared me for being able to be there at that doorway."

The couple had lived on American communes before moving to Paris in 1979 with their small daughter. At that time, Erika recalls, America was more advanced in its cultural and political revolution than Europe, but Robert felt he had more freedom there to create political art. At the time, Erika was suffering from "cultural interruptus. France was not yet aware of what later came to be known as the New Age. But, France has changed and so have I."

She says that Robert had talked about dying. "He wasn't wearing an illness, but he knew. He talked about death, his death. He told me to prepare. He said he didn't want to be old, to feel limited. It scared me. I became afraid of losing him and couldn't imagine not being with him."

Her husband was finishing up a film project when he contracted meningitis. "He thought he had the flu and stayed in bed for the weekend in terrible pain. He went into a coma which lasted for ten days before he left his body. I asked people to light candles and pray. Word spread out with the help of technology and friends around the globe were able to be with him in spirit in many languages and cultural expression. There was so much energy being released that my own life radiated with sparkling details. People kept sharing stories. Many people dreamt of Robert, felt him, and received signs."

Erika, their daughter, and two friends placed his body in a casket lined with white muslin and wrapped his body in an Indian poncho from Bolivian friends. "He looked powerful and beautiful. I gave him an eagle feather and some sage.

"Thirty years with someone is a taste. A good enough taste to not regret what you missed but understand what you had. Life is not a greedy path but an adventure. In some ways I feel more married now than when we inhabited the same dimension."

"You gain strength, courage and confidence by every experience in which you really stop to look fear in the face. . . . You must do the thing which you think you cannot do." —eleanor roosevelt

Sorry, No Miracles

Known as the "cosmetics cop," Paula Begoun says that never in her twenty-five years of writing about the cosmetics industry has she seen "such a glut of products claiming to get rid of wrinkles or firm up sagging skin." Even more shocking is how much women are spending on them. "One of the fastest-growing segments of the industry is the sale of luxury skin-care products, defined as costing more than $70 an ounce. The sad thing," says Paula, "is most women, regardless of age, political leaning, feminist sensibilities, intellectual pursuits, or business aspirations, believe these products must work and eagerly buy them."

Who has not fallen for products claiming to take years off, visibly reduce crow's-feet, give you ten years back, reverse time, and create a younger-looking you? But regrettably, she says of antiwrinkle and antiaging products, including the ones with "natural" ingredients, "None of these can live up to a modicum of the claims asserted on their labels or promised by the people selling them."

Paula is a consumer advocate, investigator, and author of *Don't Go to the Cosmetics Counter Without Me* and *Don't Go Shopping for Hair-Care Products Without Me*. She writes a syndicated newspaper advice column about cosmetics and sends out regular e-mail alerts. Her many fans won't even buy an eyeliner unless it's one of Paula's picks.

Paula's critics argue that she's not a scientist. True, but she is an investigative reporter whose rare beat is the cosmetics industry. She doesn't personally test the products ("I wouldn't have any face left," she says) but reports on ingredients, the research behind the claims.

She also sells her own line of skin-care products and cosmetics, prompting concerns over possible conflicts of interest. How can she rate other products that compete with her own? She agrees that's a bit like having Ralph Nader sign and sell his own line of cars, but she rationalizes by saying that she gives high marks and endorsements to many of her competitors.

The Seattle resident has become a recognized authority on the industry, speaking at dermatology conferences and regularly appearing on TV talk shows, having studied more fine print than most consumers have. She also has a lot to say, some hopeful, some discouraging, about aging skin.

"Growing old cannot be reversed by the right skin-care routine, by jerking your face around with elaborate exercises or by stimulating muscles with machines. As far as antiaging products are concerned, you are never going to get what you think you've paid for, unless you're buying a sunscreen, because sunscreens can truly prevent a great deal of sun damage, and that's what is primarily causing our skin to wrinkle."

Paula was already a makeup artist and knew about the basics of good skin care when she got a job at a department store makeup counter in 1977. On one of her first days she advised a customer that instead of buying an expensive toner she'd be better off picking up some hydrogen peroxide at the drugstore for fifty cents. When Paula told her manager that the cosmetic lines she was assigned to sell didn't offer the best makeup colors or skin-care products for every woman who asked about them, the manager said the customers didn't care about that. "The customers never ask questions, because they trust our products," Paula told her boss, and she ended up losing that job. She says, "Definitely I am very critical of the industry about most of their claims."

THAT SUNNY, FUNNY FACE

For sun damage, Paula Begoun says there are no miracles, but for serious maintenance, and to prevent more damage, she recommends the following:

- Retin-A or Renova, to change abnormal cell production back to some level of normalcy

- An effective AHA or BHA product, to exfoliate the top layer of the skin

- A skin-lightening product that includes at least 1 to 2 percent hydroquinone (over the counter) or 4 percent or greater (from your doctor)

- A great, reliable sunscreen, SPF 15 or greater, with the UVA-blocking ingredients titanium dioxide, zinc oxide, and/or avobenzone (or butylmethoxydibenzone), used every day for life

- A gentle cleanser, to keep the skin clean and irritant free

- A soothing, lightweight moisturizer for dry areas

As for cosmetic procedures, she says, "They've absolutely become safer and relatively cheaper over the years, and that trend will most assuredly continue. This is primarily due to the extensive antiaging research taking place, fueled by the plethora of baby boomers that have no intention of growing old 'gracefully' but who want to fight it every step of the way. As a result, there are better techniques, less-invasive procedures, and creative combinations that produce truly amazing results.

"What I do worry about is the obsession this can create. The fear of any facial flaw, at any age, causes women to over-Botox their faces into motionless masks, inject their lips into a swollen distortion, cut and paste their sags into a permanent look of surprise, and laser away their wrinkles to the point that faces start to have an eerie, plastic sameness. Hollywood celebrities have shown us how this can happen and it isn't a pretty picture."

That doesn't mean she's personally against cosmetic work. "I love Botox," she says with frankness. And she also uses a dermal injection that fills out facial lines. "I'm not nuts about my wrinkles and my gray hair. It ain't fun. I'd prefer not having them. Good skin care can ward off the amount of damage or the amount of correction needed, but there's not a cosmetic that works better than a corrective procedure." If there were, she says, cosmetic surgeons would be going out of business.

As for a goal of finding beauty in the older, cosmetically uncorrected face, she says, "Beauty as a definition is nothing more than a cultural notion. It cannot be influenced by speeches, parades, demonstrations, or editorials. A wrinkled visage is not going to start showing up on the cover of fashion magazines or the bathing suit issue of *Sports Illustrated* just because it would be politically correct.

"Despite my political or feminist bent of wanting beauty to have a deeper meaning than the obvious superficial representations, I still don't want my brows sagging on to my eyelids or my skin folding into deep creases along my face. This quandary is a reality for most women the world over and it creates confusion and frustration. The good news is that an older woman's face doesn't have to look old and it doesn't have to look pulled and yanked into a masklike contortion."

On the other hand, says the cosmetic cop, "For a woman who eschews cosmetic corrective procedures, beauty can and hopefully does evolve into style, élan, and confidence, an unmistakable energy and aura that are as powerful and compelling as any cover girl may hope to emulate."

You Want Your Face to Freeze Like That?

Y ou will know them by their goofy faces. Look over at a stoplight and see a woman trying to curl her jaw over her top lip. Or sitting at the computer wagging her nose back and forth. These women are giving themselves a free eyelid tuck or maybe a firm new profile. What's good for the glutes must also be good for the other cheeks, they reason.

Linda, a former flight attendant turned massage therapist, has been doing facial exercises for more than three years. She swears they're what tightened up a once droopy eye. "And you know those little pockets of fat on the eyelids? Some of them are gone."

She does her exercises ten minutes every day, sometimes in her car. "I can tell they're doing something because if I don't do them for a couple of days and then go back to them it feels like something is going to crack." She says it's the same tingling feeling one gets from holding any pose and then letting it go. "It makes my face brighter," she says. There's one with the jaw and the lip that she says "tightens the little thing under the neck."

Linda says, "We know that yoga can restructure the body, firm up the muscles, make the saggies go away. What I do is tone the muscles in my face." One of her favorites is squeezing her mouth tight for several seconds, holding, and letting it pop open. She says it keeps her lips in shape.

My friend Teresa the musician says you can get the same effect from playing the saxophone.

The Goldie Hawn Wave

Mollie was watching the Academy Awards and thinking about upper arm awareness. This particular year most of the beauties on the red carpet, regardless of age, felt compelled to wear something that revealed not only their cleavage and backside, but their arms. We all know about the arms. They like to make independent moves. Even the well-toned ones that look like wood carvings will every so often let out an impromptu jiggle. So Mollie started watching to see how the famous people were handling their arm presentation.

So on the night of the Oscars Mollie watched as various Hollywood stars came out and greeted their admiring fans. Some would give little-girl finger-twiddling waves. Some would give Queen Mum waves, which can be disastrous because they often set off uncontrollable upper-arm swing.

Then came Goldie Hawn, a woman as taut as anyone old enough to mother Kate Hudson. Goldie walked onto the red carpet, shot her arm straight up, and waved her hand from side to side. Imagine a little kid in the back of the classroom trying to get the teacher's attention to go to the bathroom. It was that kind of wave. A purposeful, straight-up wave that does not allow the arm to be half cocked.

Try it in front of a mirror with your shirt off. You'll be amazed that nothing (or little) moves, although you may need to practice it to get it perfect. It will be worth it. When you are next called on to walk in front of thousands and the photographers are snapping you from every possible vantage point, you will stand tall, smile broadly, and wave with purpose. And they will say of you, "All that and beautiful biceps, too."

" . . . every cover of every magazine I've done has been airbrushed to death. No woman should walk around thinking that's what they should be. You shouldn't be beating yourself up." **—teri hatcher**

HOW TO BE A HOTTIE AFTER FIFTY

It has been said of Meryl Streep, or maybe it was Teresa Heinz Kerry, that her sex appeal comes from her obvious confidence and sophistication, the same qualities that make older men sexy. With that in mind, I'd like to offer some additional hottie tips:

- Authority and experience are sexy.
- Walk with your head high. No slumping.
- Laugh like you mean it. An unabashed roar trumps a girlish giggle.
- Learn to tango for attitude and posture. Same with flamenco.
- When there's music, don't sit in your chair and wait to be asked to dance.
- Sexy women wear heels, if only in their minds. If your doctor or good sense advises sensible shoes, then buy them and wear them, but don't shuffle. Walk as if you're wearing high heels even if they're sneakers.
- Forget everything you've ever read about women of a certain age becoming invisible.
- Abandon the oversized garments. Showing a slightly rounded tummy or a real woman's hips is eminently more appealing than hiding under yards of fabric.
- Walk into a room smiling, expecting to be noticed.
- Find someone who thinks you're hot and you'll feel like a hottie.

Hello, Gorgeous

Think of someone you know who is beautiful to you. Describe her. Does age have anything to do with it? Does she look exotic or interesting? Do you notice her skin and her eyes, her long fingers? Her spirit and dignity? Do you remember the way she laughs and how she cocks her head while listening to you?

Now think about this: a male dermatologist defended bovine collagen injection despite the risk of mad cow disease by saying that more women would rather die of dementia than with wrinkles on their face. How nuts is that?

We need to prove that guy wrong.

Do you wish your mother were lovelier? Would you change your grandmother's soft face? Your sister's? Your granddaughter's?

Think of what is most beautiful about your best friend, and I bet it won't be her eyebrows that first come to mind. How about the woman next to you in choir? Look around the table at the gorgeous faces at your next family dinner. Would you change a one? Just your own, you say? Okay, well, that's the one that will take the most work.

Vieja *Isn't Old*

Isabel Allende says she doesn't have one role model for aging well, but she passes on this advice she picked up from someone she much admires: "I often think of something Sophia Loren once said in an interview. The journalist asked how Sophia managed to look so good at her age and Sophia replied something like 'I don't make old woman's noises and I walk straight.'"

Isabel adds to that list, "No coughing, no talking to myself, no sighing, and screeching when my bones ache. And I try to walk straight, mainly because I am so short that I can easily disappear in the pattern of the rug."

The Chilean hot-selling author likes to say she makes love in Spanish. She doesn't give details, but it's clear that the Spanish version is more sizzling than the English.

Isabel also makes the word *old,* which is *vieja* in Spanish, a more respectful and loving term than it is in English. She calls her mother "vieja," and that is also what her son calls her. Isabel calls her husband "mi viejo adorado," which, she says, "I'm not going to translate because in English it is absolutely corny."

In Latin families, "aging is part of life," says Isabel. "It is not burdened with negativity. However, this is changing today in urban areas, where the young pop culture imported from the USA is making a big impact." But, she adds, "Most of my Chilean friends, women over sixty, do not tint their hair and they have no problem showing their age. Most of them look great."

In her fifties she says she learned "to let go, not to try to control everything and everybody in my life. I learned to focus, to give better use to my time and my energy, not to waste myself in useless causes. I became more efficient in my work because I finally accepted that writing is the only thing that I know how to do. I also have the incredible good fortune of being in love with the man I live with."

Passing into her sixties has called for some adjustment, says Isabel. "I am learning that my energy is limited, that I have to exercise every day and eat small portions of the right stuff. I can no longer work twelve hours a day. I need leisure time. I have relaxed a lot. I want to enjoy my life, write, take care of the people I love, give something back to the community and the world. I have become a witch. I feel powerful."

AND THE WORST OF TIMES

Isabel's fifties were also filled with great sadness following the death of her daughter Paula. "She fell in a coma and died a year later. During that awful year I took care of her at home. There was very little to do, just hold her hand, wait, and remember. Very few people have the opportunity to spend a year in silence and sorrow with a broken heart. It is the most cleansing experience. The person I am today emerged from that river of tears. That was my daughter's gift to me."

Her book *Paula,* written from that experience, was her most important writing. "It saved me from suicide and my daughter from oblivion."

137

What surprises her about getting older? "I am still as passionate about life and people and causes as I was before. I could still do crazy things for love. I am still curious and adventurous. It delights me that I can have the best sex of my life and that I can share almost everything with my husband. My grandchildren also delight me and I enjoy the constant presence of my mother, who lives in Chile. We write a letter a day to each other."

The most essential aspect of aging well, she says, is health. "If one is healthy, the level of energy is high and the rest is just work and a positive attitude. What I fear about aging is dependency. I pray that I will be able to take care of myself to the last day of my life. I am so arrogant that I also want to die on my own terms."

And how does she look so good? "I get up at 6:30 A.M. and hike with my dog, the only exercise I do. I spend thirty minutes on my hair and makeup and only then I am ready for work. I write at home, so there is always the temptation to stay in my nightgown and slippers, but I still dress carefully and put on some jewelry. Without earrings I feel naked. Clothes are very important to me. I love fabrics, texture, and color and I dress in silk, velvet, light and delicate fabrics that make me feel feminine.

"I had a face-lift and I will probably have another before I turn seventy. That doesn't mean that I am clinging to youth. Aging is unavoidable. But I have a very public life and I want to look good."

"Both women and melons are best when fairly ripe."
—spanish proverb

Never the Plain Jane

J ane Fonda says she never had a role model for how to be an older woman, but in her sixties she's become one herself. If ever there were a woman practiced in reinventing herself it's this Hollywood star, savvy businesswoman, lightning-rod activist, and surprise best-selling writer. Ex-husband Ted Turner once told her, "People can't change after sixty." The old boy got that wrong. In her late sixties Jane continued her remodeling, calling it her "third act," and bringing out mostly adoring crowds to applaud her latest incarnation.

During her book blitz promoting her biography *My Life So Far,* she packed stores and auditoriums. True, one disgruntled Vietnam vet in Kansas City spat tobacco juice in her face at a book signing, but she cleaned herself off and got a standing ovation, and her book went to the top of the charts. One fan in San Francisco asked if she'd please consider running for president. (She said no.) After the book came the release of her first movie in fifteen years, *Monster-In-Law,* in which she shared the screen with Jennifer Lopez, who underscored the age difference by telling an interviewer she used to work out to Jane Fonda's videos when she was a kid.

Few women have not had their Jane Fonda period, even if it was only to cut their hair in a *Klute*-style shag and walk around in leg warmers. In many ways Jane Fonda is a living example of American women's history, from the middle of the last century to the beginning of this one. She's more of an everywoman than Gloria Steinem and other feminist icons. They gave us a political agenda, but Jane seems to have lived a life similar to our own, trying to balance all the possibilities new to women of our generation: Working mother. Driven professional. The rebel who wanted to change the world but still have superior abs.

Sure, she has exceptional good looks, talent, and privilege, but the rest of us identified with her suffering from eating disorders, marching against war, being a chameleon for a man, trying to balance motherhood and a career, and longing to be better friends with her father. Jane Fonda was not the only woman to go into therapy because of "the disease to please."

In her sixties Jane has continued to fine-tune herself—finding a spiritual life as a "liberal, feminist, progressive Christian," divorcing third husband Turner, embracing the nonglitzy life in Atlanta, becoming a philanthropist, and maintaining an important presence in her community with the teenage pregnancy program she created.

At the above-mentioned San Francisco appearance, the audience spilled out the door and around the corner. There were people of all ages, and, unusual for a book signing, there were almost as many men as women. She was due to get hip surgery soon after but gamely stepped to the podium in skinny pants and a green fitted jacket, the same lime shade as her aviator glasses. She was also as trim as she was in her go-for-the-burn period, but minus the voluptuousness, having had breast implants removed.

That she once felt the need to have big breasts to please her men and her culture and then decided that it was unhealthy bunk is another example of the personal growth she so willingly shares with the public. "It took me sixty years to realize we're not supposed to be perfect," she said in San Francisco. "What we're supposed to be is complete. Good enough is good enough."

When she talked with me by phone from Atlanta a few weeks later, I asked what kind of mature woman Jane Fonda had for her role model. Perhaps Kate Hepburn? "Maybe I'd want her looks, but not her life," she said. There was no older woman that she emulated. But she said she thinks the women of her generation are pretty good role models.

"We're seeing women of a certain age who are vibrantly on their journey that we never saw before. We're remaining healthier longer than women used to. We're physically active. We're able to extend the journey. We're everywhere. We're in the marketplace. We're involved in self-discovery. We're discovering the joy of friends and new relationships. Some of us are in transition and a little flummoxed about how to do it. But we'll continue to reinvent ourselves, hopefully until we die."

One of the reasons she went back to film work after fifteen years away from Hollywood was to make money for her teenage pregnancy prevention work in Georgia. "These are poor kids who need a reason for hope. They've been subjected to violence, racism, bad schools. We help parents become good parents, teach kids to set goals, help girls who have been abused to heal." She boasts that Georgia, once the state with the highest rate of teen pregnancy, is now number seven on the list.

For her own good health she's given up alcohol and she exercises regularly, although it's not her old brand of aerobics. "I lift weights, chop trees, move rocks, do yoga, take hikes."

Even with osteoarthritis she still moves like the agile Chelsea, her character in *On Golden Pond,* who did a back flip to please her father. In her book she writes that Katharine Hepburn, who played her mother in *On Golden Pond,* pushed Jane to do her own backward dive off the dock into the lake instead of using a stunt double. After three weeks of practice Jane did the dive and won Hepburn's respect. The actress told her, "You faced your fear. Everyone should know that feeling of overcoming fear and mastering something. People who aren't taught that become soggy."

Jane Fonda writes that Kate Hepburn was "a living testament to non-sogginess."

She could be talking about herself.

ACTING OUR AGE

Here's a starter list of hormonally compatible stars of stage and screen who make us proud. You add yours.

- Candice Bergen
- Jacqueline Bisset
- Stockard Channing
- Jill Clayburgh
- Julie Christie
- Tyne Daly
- Blythe Danner
- Judi Dench
- Jane Fonda
- Diane Keaton
- Jessica Lange
- Christine Lahti
- Helen Mirren
- Bernadette Peters
- Isabella Rossellini
- Susan Sarandon
- Sissy Spacek
- Meryl Streep
- Kathleen Turner
- Sigourney Weaver

Something Completely Different

Suddenly it's over. The music stops. The thrill is gone. You need a divorce from the job you thought you'd have forever. But how can you quit doing what you've always done? It's your identity. It's your income. You need to talk to a reinvented woman.

Stacey decided to stop being a doctor, at least the white-coated, stethoscope-in-her-pocket kind, because she wanted to express herself. "I grew up with a father who was in the Navy and the CIA. We were not an emotional family. Then I became a doctor. You can't be emotional when you're a doctor. You can't be vulnerable if you're a doctor. You have to have it all together."

Her transformation began with acting lessons. "A patient (a drama teacher) owed me money and I bartered acting classes for her bill. I'd taken drama in college. I got a C. In acting you're supposed to find and identify emotions so you can express them. I was terrible. I was wooden. I could talk and lecture, but I couldn't feel much. Nothing happened until she had me throw a tantrum, like two-year-olds do. I'd never thrown a tantrum as a child. I knew when I was little that wouldn't get me places." Stacey threw the tantrum, which led to a whole "rainbow of anger." And then other genuine stuff.

Another reason she decided to stop practicing family medicine was the cost of being a doctor. In a piece for the *Journal of the American Medical Association,* she wrote, "After a lifetime of dutiful decisions that have taken others into account before my needs I will now live a life of my own." She left an opening, saying she might return were there a change to "a kinder, gentler more effective health care system."

She explains, "I would fall in love with my patients and then have to drop an insurance plan and they'd have to go elsewhere. I was a solo physician running a business, putting out money in payroll and malpractice insurance. Taking home only enough to cover the mortgage and the taxes. One year I made less than my receptionist."

When her father died she inherited enough money to seriously consider doing something else. She joined friends on a sailboat in Mexico, weighed the pros and cons of leaving medicine, returned to California, and closed down her practice.

"I was fifty-four. Everyone said, 'You're so lucky. You're retired. You're free.' But I was at a loss. What reason did I have to get up in the morning if I didn't have patients?"

Then one day while walking, she stepped into a hole and broke her foot, ending up with even more time for self-reflection. She decided the choice was meant to be.

"My mother was creative but she couldn't act on those instincts. My father left me a nest egg. It finally made wonderful sense to me to use the money he had left so I could become the creative person my mother couldn't be."

She now performs in community theater groups, writes a medical advice column for newspapers, and is writing a book on her spiritual experiences as a baby doctor.

"The creative part may be my last career," she says. "I tend to do my life in twenty-year chunks. Maybe when I'm seventy I'll become a painter."

Let's Open Up a Bookstore

How about going into business for yourself? Running a coffeehouse. Selling imports. Writing travel stories from Florence.

Hey, how about opening your own bookstore?

It's a popular fantasy for women whose idea of bliss is hanging out in a room full of best sellers and classics, the pot on for tea, a cat sleeping in the window. Of course, the fantasy stops short of the back office where they count the money and try to keep the business afloat.

In the town of Cotati, near Sonoma State University, is North Light Books and Cafe, owned by two clever, funny women, Carolina and Barbara. Carolina, who used to be a contractor, deals with the public, which she says is like being a bartender. Lots of quick intimacy—"three minutes of heart-to-heart contact." Barbara, who used to be a teacher, hospice worker, and bookkeeper, pays the bills.

Like most independent bookstores, North Light is bleeding like a Marcia Muller thriller. So much so that one dry summer Barbara and Carolina sent letters out to friends and customers, asking for help. Come often, buy books, have lunch.

"You know how it is," says Carolina, who keeps a grim tally of bookstore closings around the country. "Everybody loves a place, and then it goes out of business and they say, 'I had no idea.'"

It worked. A new customer from twenty miles away became a regular. A pensioner in the neighborhood gave them $100. College students bought their assigned literature for humanities and English classes at the store. Encouraged, Barbara and Carolina promised to dig in for at least another year.

Despite the stresses, they say the fantasy holds. "If you're a reader, having a bookstore is nirvana," says Barbara. They opened their store on a small scale with a $50,000 SBA loan and a vision. Carolina had never touched a cash register but had come of age in Berkeley where bookstores and coffeehouses were "the acme of urban pleasure," so she had an idea of what she wanted to do.

They opened in the early 1990s, "before the bad times," says Barbara, referring to the takeover of independents by bookstore chains. Later, they moved to a new site where they could expand and add food, author readings, live music, cards, and gifts. "In this business you need sidelines," says Carolina. When things got tight they maxed out their credit cards, refinanced their houses, and took solace in the fact that "no one else is making money in this business" either. Carolina said they went to a trade show for independent booksellers. "They were all like us. Bad shoes, clunky cars."

Chain stores were only the first assault on independents. Next came Amazon.com and DSL, which make online ordering and delivery a snap for customers and clobber bookstores. "People call and want the IBSN [book code] for a book so they can order online. I won't give it to them," says Barbara.

These bookstore owners consider community support a reciprocal agreement. They hang only local art. They buy their produce from local farmers. They put on Christmas book drives for poor kids in their school district. They say that when only the bookstore chains are left there will be no one who'll take a chance on gifted new writers or support local authors. There'll be no one like Barbara insisting, "I know you and you will love this book."

MYTH: You can't teach an old dog new tricks.
FACT: First of all, you're not your cocker spaniel. In the last census, there were 344,000 women over fifty attending college. Plus 45,000 full-time female college faculty members fifty-five and older.

MYTH: They'll be putting me out to pasture pretty soon.
FACT: Three-fifths of women between the ages of fifty-five and sixty-one are working, as are two-fifths of women sixty-two to sixty-four and more than one-fifth of women ages sixty-five to sixty-nine. By 2010, 20 percent of the workforce will be fifty-five and older.

MYTH: Retirement means sitting around, doing nothing.
FACT: Eighty percent of boomers plan to work during their retirement years.

Same Passion, New Voice

For her fifty-seventh birthday Lindajoy gave herself a present: she enrolled in a class called "Taming the Inner Critic." It worked. "I've become comfortable with myself. I've decided that my life is valuable. I used to beat myself up that what I did was not important. But I'm comfortable being a behind-the-scenes person. I did it as a reporter. I'm doing it now in the music world. I do it well and I know I've left my mark."

Several surprising things happened to Lindajoy at middle age. She changed jobs after thirty years in journalism and became a music manager. And she learned to speak her mind.

First, she stopped being a journalist in the traditional sense, after working for years as a Mexican correspondent for American media. She still writes, but now she does so for publications that seek her opinions and expertise in a field that she developed by happenstance.

Next, she became a music manager, a job that resulted from her using her nose for news. It started when she was going through old music racks in a Mexico City store and found a tape of violinist Juan Reynoso. She immediately fell in love with his homegrown "calentana" music, folk melodies of the Tierra Caliente region, and decided she needed to find him, "just to meet him and thank him for his music."

Using her reporter skills, she tracked him down. They became friends and she talked Reynoso, then in his eighties, into doing a concert that she would produce. That concert evolved into an annual festival celebrating regional Mexican musicians.

She also persuaded him to take his music to the United States and introduce traditional Mexican music to Americans at venues like the Olympic Music Festival in the Pacific Northwest. The Mexican government ended up giving Reynoso the country's highest honor for an artist, the National Arts and Science Award.

These days Lindajoy lives both in Mexico City and in California but spends most of her time on the road with a number of different folk musicians representing different countries. Occasionally she takes time off to play a little fiddle, mandolin, and guitar herself.

As part of her new life she's also enjoying expressing her opinion. "As a journalist we're trained to be objective. When you're a reporter or an editor you don't want people knowing what you think. You need to avoid taking a public stand. So you don't tell people what you believe. But now I get to talk like real people."

Lindajoy has a role model who helps her believe that good changes in her life will continue. This New York friend at eighty-nine "is still making music and still getting mad about politics. She reads the newspaper every morning and jumps up and down. It's reassuring."

Be Aware of All Options

Boomers have helped make the kitchen almost as sexy as the bedroom, falling in love with all things culinary, trying new cuisine, and requiring esoteric utensils their mothers never had in their cabinets. And Martha Stewart is not the only woman who has made a career catering to the rediscovery of domestic joys. Kathy Tierney, CEO of Sur La Table, the Seattle-based kitchen retailer, says that's why she likes her stores "to have a sense of discovery, like going to a foreign bazaar."

The creative part of retailing is what Kathy enjoys best, although she's obviously skilled at running the whole operation. Kathy joined Sur La Table in her late fifties by way of Smith & Hawken, the Nature Company, and the Himalayas. "I get questions from young women asking for advice on becoming successful. I tell them I never had a plan, but it's important to always be aware of your options." It's worked for her to follow her heart and her gut and take advantage of each detour. "At the time you'll do something which doesn't seem important, but you look back and see how it led you to something remarkable."

When she was a young mother her husband won a Fulbright scholarship, allowing him to study in England. She and their son, then in the third grade, went along. "I loved Thomas Hardy so I thought I'd go live in a rose-covered cottage and read. But then I got involved in English gardening, with no idea what was ahead for me."

Years later, in the early 1990s, her passion for gardening helped position her to take over as chief executive for Smith & Hawken. "It was never a plan, like I'll get my MBA, work at one particular place for two years and then move up. For me, it was, oh, wow, I love gardening."

Before taking the helm at Smith & Hawken, she helped run the Nature Company, a job she obtained through friends she met while working in the Peace Corps. And before that she was a teacher. Even so, she says she didn't really start focusing on her career until she was thirty-eight.

In her fifties she quit her job at Smith & Hawken and took a long work break after her brother-in-law, also in his fifties, suddenly died. "I said, 'There's a bunch of things I want to do.' I was in a comfortable situation but I had to move on." She took a year off and with her sister and son went to Asia, India, Australia, New Zealand, Laos, and Cambodia. After that huge trip she took off again with her mother, who was in her eighties and wanted to see Africa.

"I called it my sabbatical year. It was real important for me to do, especially in my fifties. If I hadn't taken that break I wouldn't have had the energy to do what I do now."

One of her dreams was to hike in the Himalayas, which she attempted. Unfortunately she ended up in a Katmandu hospital with internal bleeding, a result of altitude sickness and dengue fever. But she needed to do it, she says. "It was one of those heart feelings, you know, when someone talks about doing something and your heart aches because you want to do it too. It could be anything."

Kathy intends to mark her sixtieth birthday by sailing the Pacific with her husband, although she says she has no plans to stop working in the near future. But she's thought about what she won't do whenever she does retire. "I don't think a person wants to ever retire from life. I will always want to be engaged in some way, to be involved in something I care about, to feel connected to what's going on. When you're not engaged, people don't value your opinions as much. You're discounted. You need to stay part of society. It may be different in other places, but our society doesn't value people who sit around and just think. I've always thought I'd like to grow old like Monet, to garden and paint. But I'm not a painter. Maybe I'll garden and write a book."

Living in Seattle, where the winter days are short, Kathy has to push herself to get the exercise she's always made a priority. She brings in a yoga teacher twice a week for her and her staff. She's been running for twenty-five years and she also skis. In the summer she and her sisters hike in the Sierra Nevada mountains, from the top of Donner Summit to Squaw Valley. "Every year we say no matter how old we get we will make sure we do this."

Who Would Have Thought?

Former English teacher Barbara Bickmore became a Cinderella-style success at age fifty-four when she wrote her first novel. Some reviewers call her books "romantic yarns" and use adjectives like "steaming" to describe stories "chock-full of passion, secrets, murders and lies," but Barbara does not accept the label of romance novel being attached to her books.

"I do not write romance. I take an average woman, throw slings and arrows at her, and make her grow," says Barbara, who lives in Eugene, Oregon. One story is set in Oregon, but most are based in Africa, Australia, China, and England.

She started writing when she was seven years old but she didn't try to sell what she wrote until she had given up teaching, moved to Oregon to farm, failed at that, and ended up "stone cold broke. I couldn't afford gas to drive downtown to get my food stamps."

Sounding like one of her characters, she says, "I began writing to escape my plight." What she did was go to the library and read books on how to get published. "I treated it as a business, not an art. To write genre was the easiest way to make money. I didn't care about science fiction. I wasn't clever enough to write mysteries. Romances made me sort of vomit but I thought, 'I can do that.'"

She took a class from a writer who praised her first attempt and gave her the name of his agent. The agent told her she wrote far too well for romance and advised her to write something with more meat. *East of the Sun,* her first book, is the story of a young missionary woman who goes to Africa, stays for six decades, and witnesses racial clashes, famine, and the beginning of the AIDS epidemic. Its success earned her a $300,000 advance on her next two books.

"I'm unbelievably fortunate," says Barbara, who is long divorced and lives alone because she can't write with anyone else in the house. Now in her seventies, she says, "age has nothing to do with success in writing. I went to Europe on a speaking tour and worried that they'd see how old I am and wouldn't like me. They were charmed and delighted. Europe told me I was lovely and wonderful and asked when my next book was coming out."

All of her heroes are women. "They're not selfless. They're not Mother Teresa. But they contribute to the world. I like men and I know very nice men. But it made me so damned mad that only men got to be heroes. I was a feminist before I heard the word."

Book Babes and Juicy Titles

Novelist Meredith Blevins, who writes about lusty women often beyond the first blush, tells of an agent who read her first book, *The Hummingbird Wizard,* and thought he might do something with it. "He wrote me a glowing letter and said he was handing it to his assistant to get a woman's point of view." That killed it, Meredith says, because the woman, who was in her late twenties, read the manuscript and was surprised to find that the main character was pushing fifty. She said something like "Quite frankly, the idea that someone would blow on her inner thighs really grossed me out. And it would certainly not be marketable."

The agent turned down the book. Fortunately, others didn't, and Meredith's career has flourished. But it gives us an idea of what we're up against when we try to find ourselves in literature.

Despite this difficulty, there are books whose authors know how to tell the truth about women of experience, who are strong, feisty, and sometimes funny as hell. Here's a sampling:

RIPE WOMEN, LUSCIOUS TALES

The Amateur Marriage by Anne Tyler. An extraordinary account of an ordinary long-lasting marriage.

The Distinguished Guest by Sue Miller. Lily, a literary superstar, now must rely on the kindness of family and strangers.

Drinking the Rain by Alix Kates Shulman. This longtime urban writer tells about living simply and alone on her piece of an island in Maine.

Floating in My Mother's Palm by Ursula Hegi. Hanna's mother is a reckless artist who dares her to swim in a thunderstorm.

Graced Land by Laura Kalpakian. A welfare mother is addicted to Elvis.

Having Our Say: The Delany Sisters' First 100 Years by Sarah and A. Elizabeth Delany. Daughters of a former slave share their life and wisdom, including "Life is short and it's up to you to make it sweet."

Homestead by Rosina Lippi. A generation of amazing women live through war in an Austrian village.

The House by the Sea: A Journal by May Sarton. In an oceanfront house in Maine, Sarton observes the seasons, tends her garden, pours a glass of wine, and studies the sea.

The Jane Austen Book Club by Karen Joy Fowler. Austen addicts pass around marital advice and margaritas and also deliver a good primer on *Pride and Prejudice* and other Austen works.

Liza's England by Pat Barker. There's more than tea and politics in the life of an eighty-four-year-old woman.

The Master Butchers Singing Club by Louise Erdrich. Love, sex, death, and two women drinking beer in the night stretch the boundaries of a small town in North Dakota.

The Matisse Stories by A. S. Byatt. A rosy nude painting lures a woman into a beauty salon, and other stories.

Miss Garnet's Angel by Salley Vickers. A retired British history teacher finds art and adventure in Venice.

My Dream of You by Nuala O'Faolain. An Irish travel writer moves to the country to discover her history and a tender, generous lover.

Oldest Living Confederate Widow Tells All by Allan Gurganus. A feisty thinking woman shares her take on the Civil War and marriage to a much older man.

The Prize Winner of Defiance, Ohio by Terry Ryan. A clever mother supports her family by coming up with money-making jingles in the 1950s.

Revenge of the Middle-Aged Woman by Elizabeth Buchan. Husband leaves and she's canned. Can you guess who wins?

The Seven Sisters by Margaret Drabble. Alone and pitiful in the beginning, a woman receives inheritance money and takes her friends to Naples.

Spending: A Utopian Divertimento by Mary Gordon. This might be every woman's fantasy—a muse who cooks as well as he makes love.

Stones for Ibarra by Harriet Doerr. An Anglo couple moves to a Mexican village and for a time get to live their dream.

Terms of Endearment by Larry McMurtry. Aurora Greenway, who also figures in *The Evening Star,* is a bit temperamental but generous and full of grace.

A Walk on the Beach: *Tales of Wisdom from an Unconventional Woman* by Joan Anderson. Two women meet on the beach in Cape Cod and share life's experiences and surprises.

A Widow for One Year by John Irving. A mother's demons drive her to many things, some unacceptable, some quite luscious.

Walking to the Metro

In her fifties Joan Samuelson appeared regularly before Congress, was portrayed in a TV movie, and joined a California commission considered so powerful that it is expected to save lives. Hopefully one of those will be Joan's.

Joan is the founder of the Parkinson Action Network, a patient advocacy and lobbying group that since 1991 has been demanding more money for Parkinson's disease research from the U.S. government. Once thought of as an old person's disease, Parkinson's struck Joan when she was thirty-six, an avid runner, a promising lawyer, and a newlywed. The disease would eventually alter all three of those aspects of her life, including contributing to the end of her marriage. But Joan used her intellect and energy to form the Parkinson Action Network and has become its most tireless advocate on Capitol Hill.

For a time she worked with actor Michael J. Fox, who also has the disease, combining his fund-raising power with her patient advocacy. Joan became a familiar face in the halls of Congress, buttonholing members and persuading them to vote for more research money for Parkinson's and staging glitzy fund-raisers. It's been exciting and frustrating.

"I've got this army invading me, and what is my country doing to save me?" she asks. For years people with Parkinson's have been told that a cure is just around the corner, but it's been held up by the ethical and political questions over stem cell therapy. In the meantime some of Joan's best friends have died as Joan likely will, if there is no intervention. One of those friends was Milly Kondracke, whose struggle with Parkinson's was featured in the TV movie, *Saving Milly*. Of the actress who played Joan's lobbyist character, she says, "I liked her, but she didn't look like she had any Parkinson's symptoms."

It usually takes an hour every morning for Joan's body to respond to her medications and begin moving. Other times she's "frozen for days." Yet she remains upbeat, funny, ironic, and loving life. A stylish woman with an easy laugh, she studies tai chi, holds musical parties in her home, and counts Tina Turner among her role models for aging outrageously.

Because of Parkinson's Joan has ended up trying to change laws rather than practice law, and she says, "I've had the most incredible professional life." After California approved Proposition 71 authorizing $3 billion in state bonds to invest in stem cell research by the state's best scientists, Joan was appointed to the high-powered body established to guide that research. "It is the right job at the right time for me. It's so heady to be able to actually change something. If we do this well it will be revolutionary. We will get the cure."

But Parkinson's is not Joan's whole life and now, in her fifties, she's trying to expand her interests. "Work and activism have always been foremost in my life. I have a very rich professional life, but I want to have a three-dimensional life—to go to more movies and have dinner with friends, to send out Christmas cards, to have someone special in my life."

One positive thing about having a debilitating condition, says Joan, is that you reassess what you think you need in life to make you happy. "I once went to a very expensive fund-raiser where the conversation centered on the decline in first-class travel. I've decided that being rich does not necessarily give people great joy."

What gives Joan great joy? She was in DC and had a dinner date across town. She could have taken a taxi, but she chose to get there under her own power, no small goal for someone who walks with a limp and whose body can stiffen without warning. But she determinedly hiked several blocks to the Metro, changed trains, went up and down stairs, got to the restaurant, had dinner, and got herself back home.

"That night I decided I'm going to walk because I can, and I have a desperate need to keep trying. I was so grateful to experience the simple joy of walking to the Metro."

Even though Joan has Parkinson's, she also dyes her hair, looks forward to the next man in her life, worries about her weight, and is willing to spend too much money on a hip pair of glasses. Plus, she's menopausal. So are lots of women with cancer, MS, heart conditions, and spinal cord injuries. "Illness happens," says Joan. "It's life. It's just another piece in navigating these years." And, she insists, it's no reason to put someone with a severe medical condition in a separate category. "It's a seamless thing," explains Joan. "Being in my fifties, trying to navigate through this period of time, I'm like every other woman. Parkinson's is just one of the pieces. It's not the whole deal. The day it becomes the whole deal is when it kills me."

Joan tells about the time the then attorney general Janet Reno, who also has Parkinson's, gave the press a quick lesson on her limitations as perceived by others. "The media had asked her about the tremor in her hand and she said something like, 'You guys are the ones obsessed with Parkinson's, not me. So I have this tremor. Get over it.'"

Joan feels the same way. "When I was diagnosed I believed that my life was over as I knew it. But it wasn't," she says. "I'm still me. Parkinson's is my elephant in the living room. But I am no different from you and every other woman living now at this age."

She knows that people look at her and worry about their own vulnerability. What if that happened to me? What would I do? Joan's answer is "When you get a diagnosis of a major illness and you survive, it makes you free. All things are then possible. Life doesn't end. You can lose your job. You can lose many things and survive."

So She Danced

Of course Geri Jewell approves of what she calls the "brutal honesty" of the *Deadwood* TV series in which she plays Jewel, the saloon's scrubwoman. She's lived fifty years with the brutal honesty of a disability. "I was told we're all made in God's image, so

I grew up thinking that God had cerebral palsy, too," she likes to say when giving speeches, to help put audiences at ease.

Geri first became known in the 1980s when she won a role on the sitcom *Facts of Life,* becoming the first disabled actor to appear in a network series. After that she had some movie parts and did stand-up comedy. Then in 2004 came *Deadwood,* the HBO Western series set in 1876 in which Geri plays Jewel, a woman with a bad leg. Her character doesn't have cerebral palsy because, as Geri explains, "cerebral palsy wasn't medically defined back then. I'm just known as the town gimp. If someone called me that today I wouldn't stand for it, but that's what they called people like me back then."

On the show Geri's curly brown hair is knotted in a bun, she wears a torn dress, and there's usually a smudge of dirt on her face. In our interview she's dressed in white jeans and pink high-top sneakers and talking about using Botox for pain, not wrinkle, relief and turning fifty in a business that usually seeks out the "young, the pretty, and the perfect."

"I didn't get famous for being a sex symbol so I don't have to worry about what a lot of actresses do. I got famous for having CP. I have the same challenges of every actress getting older but I have something that gives me an edge. In *Deadwood* my CP gives a sort of unique quality to Jewel, sets her apart, and yet her essence is that even though she's different she has the same pain and joys as anyone else."

Geri started doing stand-up comedy in nightclubs when she was twenty-one but she knew she was funny from the time she was a little girl. "It's my way of being accepted. I knew very young that people would like me if I made them laugh. Humor was my way to bridge the gap between me and the other kids."

When she was in school, disabled students were segregated into special education classes rather than mainstreamed, and Geri says that that made her emotionally younger than her peers.

"I was always very intelligent but I lacked the socialization and was about ten emotionally until I got to college. Maybe that's why I still look thirty," she quips.

When she was a kid she fantasized about being a famous rock star or actress. "I didn't go to football games or dances. I had my creative visualization to keep me alive. But in my fantasy I never had CP. That didn't hit me until after I had achieved some success, realizing that when I imagined myself famous I didn't imagine myself with a disability. Then in the 1980s I started to be known as the disabled superstar, an icon for people with disabilities. I had to learn to accept that part of me and move forward instead of saying to myself, why can't I be normal?"

As she moves into her fifties she says, "I'm just now feeling the joy and sweetness of life and the challenge." Her goal for the next ten years is "to keep growing spiritually, to have someone special in my life again, and to continue to be challenged as an artist." She's learned to count on the occasional miracle. After going through a difficult surgery and recovery from an addiction to painkillers, Geri was waiting in a Santa Monica pharmacy one day when David Milch, the director, also waiting in line, asked if she was doing any acting. What would she think about being in a Western? asked Milch, who was putting together his *Deadwood* cast.

A big acting challenge in *Deadwood* was a scene in which Jewel teaches the town's doc to dance. "Anyone who knows me knows I would never be on a dance floor. The director didn't ask ahead of time if I knew how to dance. Not only did I have to dance but I had to make it beautiful. If I had said no, they could have said 'Bye, bye, Geri. What kind of actress are you?'

"I am a professional. So I danced. And people still stop me on the street and say 'I loved you in that dance scene.'"

An Upside-Down Approach

Often when she's been cramped up in an airplane too long Ruth Mankin goes to the back of the plane and does a standing forward fold, bending at the waist and wrapping her hands behind her heels. "You can do a lot of yoga while waiting for the bathroom," says Ruth. This is an example of what Ruth means when she says we need to take yoga with us into our life.

Ruth began doing yoga in her late twenties, studying with Erich Schiffmann, the California surfer who became a world-famous yoga instructor and author. Yoga has served her well for thirty years. She's studied around the world, leads yoga tours to places like Bali, credits yoga for keeping her bones strong after menopause, and is a lush example of how beautifully the body can bend when, like hers, it's "bigger than [that of] most skinny yogis."

Yoga is a lifetime discipline, according to Ruth. "You're always a student in yoga. There is always something more to try, some place deeper to go." She plans to be like the old yogis who in their eighties can still hold a back bend for fifteen minutes at a time. "You're as young as your spine," Ruth tells her students.

She credits yoga with helping her heal some bulging discs and keeping her mind clear enough to raise two teenagers and commute two hours to a public school job every day. She's also seen yoga change others. One student "in her late fifties had been taking yoga for years but was afraid of an elbow stand. She was physically capable but her mind was in the way. People have a lot of fear about going upside down. Two of us helped her up and she just stayed there for a while. She was stunned and so happy, like a little kid who has finally stayed up on a bicycle. A little while later she asked to do it a second time. She said if she never did an elbow stand again she would always be able to say 'I did it twice.'"

Ruth begins each day by going into an elbow stand or a headstand. "I like being upside down, being balanced and looking at the world in a different way." Upside-down poses help to recirculate the blood, quiet the mind, help with migraines and indigestion, and, Ruth promises, "produce a great feeling of elation."

Ruth started taking yoga only for the exercise. "I told my teacher, 'I'm from New York, I'm not interested in the meditation stuff. I'm only here for the physical.' He laughed and said okay. Years later I understood why he laughed." Now she takes time out almost every day to sit and breathe. Those deep ocean breaths, the ones that make you sound like Darth Vader. Maybe for only a few minutes, but always going for the stillness, the inner listening, the same goal as that of the yogis thousands of years before who developed poses as a way to mediate. Controlled, watchful breathing brings oxygen to the blood and the brain and calms the mind. Ruth tells her students that when they are feeling anxious over some personal problem or a challenge at work they should stop and breathe. It worked for her during an earthquake in Los Angeles. "The room started to shake and I started breathing and then I imagined my teacher breathing with me."

Now she's using yoga principles to deal with her feelings associated with an empty nest. "I love having teenagers all over the house. I love their angst and brilliance. But pretty

RUTH'S REMINDERS

- Listen to your body.

- Lead with your heart.

- Make every movement beautiful and strong.

- You're as young as your spine.

- Remember to breathe.

soon I'll be alone in the house. I'm trying to remember that there's a lot of language in yoga about attachment and letting go. So now I'm focusing on bringing new life into my life. I have a piece of paper on my mirror that says, "Change to make change."

Maybe she'll change jobs, or take an acting class, or get back into painting, or, like the perpetual student, go to India, sit at the bare feet of the wise ones. "My teacher said if you open your mind to possibilities your body will follow."

Sweat, Baby, Sweat

Many may remember a time when it was considered unladylike to work on our bodies, never mind our brains, except for the purpose of making them pleasing to men. But look at us now. We lift weights. We carry a gym bag. We sweat. We brag about our deltoids.

Bobbie Elzey from Atlanta remembers her college days when she had to conceal her gym clothes with a coat while crossing the campus to go play on the hockey team. Was that about modesty? Those old green gym suits with the skirts were hardly revealing. Or was it because if you looked too much like an athlete people would think you didn't like men?

I thought about that concept while stopping at the gas station after my aerobics class one morning—how unconcerned I am about being seen in public in a thong leotard and tights. Whom would I offend? Certainly not the gray-haired jock racing down the hill in bicycle shorts and running bra.

The terrific news about exercise, in any form, is that if you do it smart, it works for you. It may not produce glutes as hard as cantaloupes, but it will give you even better things. Like strength, vitality, grace, agility, and balance. What do you really value in a body? All that or perky breasts?

160

Bobbie Elzey has been teaching fitness classes, mostly in the South, since the late 1970s. She recalls going to a YMCA in Atlanta when she first moved from Baltimore. "I knocked on the door and said, 'I teach aerobic dance,' and they said, 'We're not interested in belly dancing.'" She convinced them that aerobics had nothing to do with veils and finger cymbals, and they let her teach. Three people came to her first class. "Then it exploded," she says, and she was soon teaching aerobic dance instruction to YMCA fitness teachers throughout the South.

She continues to heed her calling, has the stamina and body to prove it, and is often amazed at how well exercise works. "I see women become fit so fast they're suddenly able to carry a big bag of groceries better than they did three weeks before."

When Bobbie talks about her students, many of whom have become good friends in the way that happens in exercise classes, she says it's the older ones who dazzle her with their vitality and their enthusiasm. "Southern women are so charming and reserved but a lot of them want to break out of the mold. I have one woman in class who's ninety. She has white hair and steel blue eyes and looks maybe in her late sixties. Another one is eighty and she's dancing all over the gym. She used to sing with her husband's band and she loves to move to music."

FLEX APPEAL

There are many good reasons to get thee to a gym. If you've never been athletic, you get to finally have something to say when asked what you do for exercise. You can answer, "I work out." It'll make you feel like you're in the game, jock-like even. Before long you'll be talking about strengthening your core and swearing that Pilates made you taller.

The thing about exercise is you don't have to excel to see results. You don't need to compete, run races, hit a ball, or pay for lessons. If you're dance deprived you can take an aerobics or dance exercise class and shake a tail feather to loud music. This is the place where you can pick up some hip-hop moves, but where they also still do the pony and the twist.

NOT YOUR MOTHER'S SWEATPANTS

Another benefit of doing exercise? There are endless shopping ops for fitness buffs. Karate pants. Tai chi–style pajamas. Spinning shorts and cycling shirts with back pockets for your water bottles. You can wear black tights and a pink leotard just like you did in ballet classes when you were a little girl. Or you can get as stylish as you want, depending on the gym. Go Lycra or all cotton. Or you can choose a facility where they let you show up with your hair all crooked and wearing your husband's old sweatshirt, as long as you have on proper sneakers.

Dancing improves balance, says Bobbie. "After age twenty most of us start to lose the ability to balance well. When you're a kid you're using your balance all the time, walking on a fence or along a curb. Then we stop." Bobbie has her students do an exercise in which they close their eyes and walk with one foot in front of the other like they're on a tightrope. "As people get older their base of support becomes wider. That's why you see a lot of people shuffling," and this exercise helps to narrow the base of support they need.

"Back when women started exercising the goal was to look better. Now it's to feel better. When you feel good about your body, you feel freer. It's liberating. I think what many of us fear about getting older is becoming dependent. But when you know you are building your strength it makes you feel independent."

We didn't used to understand this. We thought that once the body started to go it was a downhill slide. Nothing improved with age, except for maybe wine and cheese. But now we know it can be our muscles and bones.

"You do not automatically lose strength when you age," says Bobbie. "You can actually regain muscle and bone. When we first started doing aerobics we did little strength training, but then we realized there has to be some weights. It can't be just cardio. The body needs to be signaled that we're using it.

Bone is live tissue. It breaks down when we're not calling on it to work."

Exercise in general also helps reduce stress, raise endorphins, and keep you focused. Not only does it make you move, but it also teaches you how to relax and stretch. You could actually end up with a more agile and reliable body than you had when you were in your forties. You might still have some loose skin where you don't want it, but you'll be moving with grace and confidence.

Bobbie Elzey is her own good example of what can happen when you stay fit. At fifty-seven she got to play Peter Pan. She has acting experience, but the flying coach who rigged performers up to soar across the stage in a harness was skeptical about whether Bobbie could do it. "She's how old?" he asked the director. But Bobbie convinced him and flew for the run of the play. "I smacked into a few walls in the beginning and had a few bruises. But it was thrilling to be lifted off the stage and fly. And to sing at the same time."

Like jock talk? A gym is also a good place to pick up gossip, dip into a political debate over the plan to widen the local freeway, share excess zucchini from your garden, and make friends. For people who work from home it can be the one place they see another human being in the flesh—and so much of it.

"No one has the right to sit down and feel hopeless. There's too much work to do" **—dorothy day**

163

What Makes Judy Run

"I never worry about what I eat," declares Judy, sitting down with a coffee drink full of foam and a thick slab of banana bread. She goes on, "Do you know how many problems you can solve running side by side with a friend? Do you know how many different kinds of people I've met through training? Do you know how good it feels to be able to move your own living room furniture around?"

All I had asked was "What do you like so much about running?"

For Judy, a schoolteacher, the bigger question is why wouldn't a person run or walk or do some form of regular exercise. "If women knew how good it feels to be out there, how focused it makes you and what a relief it is to forget all that chatter in your head, they'd be out swarming the streets."

Okay, she's a little more compulsive than most, talking about "getting in five miles between appointments." But how many sixty-year-olds do you know who do the Boston marathon and the Ironman triathlon, teach second graders, have a part-time sales job, are married, have grandchildren, and are the same size (four) they were in high school?

Calling herself an athlete delights Judy because she never thought she would do anything unusually physical. In high school she had scoliosis and had to be in a special PE class for disabled kids. Along with that, "there wasn't much back then for girls in the way of sports. Cheerleading and maybe a little bit of tennis. The only people who exercised were fat people trying to lose weight, not skinny people like me."

Then the jogging craze struck and everyone was starting to run. Judy was in her thirties and her neighbor asked her to run around the block with him. "He was trying to quit smoking. The first time we ran one block. Then we did four. Four blocks equaled a mile. I couldn't believe I could cover a whole mile. I felt so accomplished."

Then she did a 5K run. "We all got ribbons. I was suddenly part of a brand-new world." Several 5Ks led to many 10Ks, and pretty soon she "kind of got sucked into" running a marathon with some other mothers. After that she watched a triathlon on TV and got sucked in deeper, but because she could only do the running part of the triathlon, she had to find someone else to swim and another person to bicycle as a team. "They were great. I was mediocre." But the trio came in first, and Judy decided her next challenge would be to do the whole thing herself.

"But all I could do was dog paddle and I didn't have a bike." So she signed up for a swimming class ("I was in the beginners' lane where you put your face in the water and blow bubbles") and bought a ten-speed bike for $100. "I'm kind of task oriented," she adds, unnecessarily.

It's more important to her to participate than to win, she says, although she has a roomful of ribbons, plaques, and shiny statues in her home. She made eight attempts before qualifying for the Ironman triathlon in Hawaii, which she did at age fifty. That was a big goal, and so was running the Boston marathon, but in general she just likes to run.

Judy says running helped her put her teaching job in perspective with her health and the rest of her life. "With teaching you become so involved, and if you get too involved it's depleting. You have to jump into your job with both feet and know when to jump out." Her routine was to run before going to her classroom, and swim or bicycle after school. "They're used to seeing me at school with a big gym bag."

She admits, "Most people are not as intense and focused as I am. You don't have to be. Just get out every day for a little bit and use your body." The perks are manifold. "The more physically involved you get the more independent you feel. You become more outspoken. You become more lively and attractive, not so much in the beauty way but because you have energy and that's appealing."

Hitting menopause at age fifty-five was "like nothing," she says. "I had hot flashes, but I'm used to sweating." Also at fifty-five her running times started to drop, but, she says, "Slower times don't

- Sudden numbness or weakness of the face, arm, or leg, especially on one side of the body
- Sudden confusion; trouble speaking or understanding
- Sudden trouble seeing in one or both eyes
- Sudden trouble walking, dizziness, loss of balance or coordination
- Sudden severe headache with no known cause

If you have any of these warning signs, call 911.

bother me. Slowing down is part of living." Slow is relative. She plans to always run, bicycle, or at least vigorously walk the dog.

"I know women who are in their seventies and do my kind of exercise. My mother at ninety-one was addicted to the treadmill. You know how getting a good haircut makes you feel good? This feels better, and it's free."

Left-Handed Painting

You can tell by looking at Lindy Lange Grant's paintings that she's lived large. The women are luscious. The men are dashing. A self-portrait done in her late forties shows a blonde beauty in a cabana chair poised for a kiss. Her people have style and moxie, I say. Lindy smiles and nods. Lindy had a stroke when she was fifty-five, six months after she and her husband moved into a country home in Northern California, a place that would turn out to be well suited for a wheelchair.

It was a typical morning, and Lindy was getting ready to leave the house. When she didn't call out to say good-bye, her husband looked into the living room and found her leaning against the couch and struggling to move. The stroke was "a big one," her husband says, which put Lindy in the hospital for five weeks.

Four years after her stroke, she's coming back, making the kind of improvements that give her and her family hope. Her husband reports, "The other day we were out walking and Lindy looked down and said, 'Mushrooms.' That's pretty amazing, seeing as how two years ago she couldn't say my name."

Lindy started painting when she was a young girl, inspired by her artist father. After formally studying art she moved to London with her first husband and children and began painting the characters she saw on the street and in cafes. Her work caught on and she was invited to do gallery shows in England, Greece, and Thailand. Photos of Lindy at her last gallery opening before the stroke show a radiant woman in white silk and red shoes drinking champagne and chatting with collectors eager to pay $3,000 to $4,000 for her paintings. Back then Lindy talked to an interviewer about the uncertainty of how an artist's work is received by the public. "I can never predict the outcome," she said. "It might be a success or a disaster." Almost prophetically, she said it takes courage to be an artist, "to keep going against all odds and not let life and people's opinions get you down."

The stroke paralyzed her right side, including her painting hand. But recently Lindy started painting again, this time with her left hand, and presented a show of her works at the Santa Rosa City Hall gallery. It was her post-stroke coming-out

And if you think someone else is in trouble and could be having a stroke, do the following:

- Ask her or him to smile.
- Ask her or him to raise both arms.
- Ask her or him to speak a simple sentence.

If the person cannot do any of these three tasks, call 911 and describe the symptoms.

party. She said little but smiled and hugged friends and family who came from Los Angeles, New York, and London. She sold eight pieces.

Lindy and her husband measure her progress by each piece of medical equipment they can move to the garage. She's down to using a wheelchair for getting around airports. The two get out as much as possible, to movies and restaurants, theater in San Francisco. Lindy's daughters take her power shopping.

Lindy calls the stroke "a big bummer" and says what she misses the most is reading books. But she believes that ability will return. She's able to read menus and flip through a reading workbook that she and her speech therapist have customized. In addition to doing both physical therapy and speech therapy, Lindy regularly flies to Palm Desert, California, to take classes at a stroke activity center. It was there that a man came up to her and said, "We all get better, you know."

That's what keeps Lindy and her family hopeful. "It's a slow, slow process," says her husband, "but Lindy is coming uphill all the time. A stroke is different from other illnesses where you keep going downhill. With this, you keep getting better, little by little," to which Lindy cries out victoriously, "Ta . . . daaah!"

Now I Know Who I Am

The only comment my mother made about the Alzheimer's disease that would end up imprisoning her for more than ten years was "I don't want to hear anything bad." That was in the early years, when things were going terribly wrong but she could still talk. My father, my sister, and I agreed to be accomplices in her denial. We would give her clues to help her, whisper the names of grandchildren as they walked up for a hug. We didn't know much about Alzheimer's. It wasn't yet widely known as a disease that would clobber so many families, hunt down a former president, and silence numerous celebrities.

My father died, leaving money that might have otherwise provided an easy and comfortable life for my mother. She had a great capacity for fun and would have had a gay time in her golden years. Instead all the gold went toward paying for a nursing home.

I wonder what other arrangement she might have made for herself had she known early about her disease and been able to plan ahead. She might have set herself up better, gone to groups to learn ways to deal with her disease like people can today.

My sister and I envisioned taking turns having her live with our families, half the year in California, half in Massachusetts. It didn't work out, though, because it was too confusing for Mom, and because we came to understand that moving a person with Alzheimer's to unfamiliar places is one of the worst things you can do for her. So is placing her in the middle of a busy household. Her needs were round the clock and neither my sister nor I could afford to stop working to care for her. So we eventually placed Mom in a nursing home, because there seemed no other options that would allow us to keep her safe and cared for.

Had my mother been able to design an ideal situation for herself, I think she would have kept her piano and as much independence as she could afford to buy. She would have had a place that had a garden, or at least a balcony where she could water her plants and put her face in the sun. Had we known more we might have had an opportunity to help her plan and talk about what she wanted to happen if she worsened and there was no hope for a cure. My sister and I tell each other we did our best, but we regret we couldn't do more.

I think about Alzheimer's a lot, just as friends dread the heart disease or MS or cancer that took their mother or father. We all have those moments when we think, "Oh no, I'm next."

Something is going to get us eventually. At the same time my mother's mind was slipping away, a friend's mother had a stroke and then fell and broke her hip. She never mended and spent her last years in a wheelchair, part of her body frozen. My friend's mother's mind stayed clear, unlike my mom's, but from the neck down she was a mess. I remember wondering which would be worse, but I think I know.

My mother and I look alike. I once caught my reflection in a train window and my first thought was "That woman looks like my mother." Once when I went to visit her in the nursing home I found her bent over and staring into cupped hands. She looked up at me and smiled slowly. "Now I know who I am," she said.

When my sister called to tell me that Mom had died, she said, "It's over." The call came in the middle of a winter storm that was pushing redwood trees around and snapping power lines across the state. I later imagined that was my mother's spirit passing through, slamming the door on her way out.

Work That Brain

No one knows what causes Alzheimer's. It could be genetic. It could be environmental. Because it is now so common—twice as many cases as there were when my mother was diagnosed in the 1980s—you can't help but wonder if it's an obvious culprit that we're not seeing. Maybe it's in the lightbulbs or the peanut butter, and one day we will know and stop losing people this way.

Several friends have lost their parents to Alzheimer's. We make nervous jokes about how name tags should be a social requirement. We hate the term "senior moment." Some of us would have kept taking estrogen even with all its health risks if studies had shown it would help prevent Alzheimer's. Instead we eat our broccoli and berries and take the latest vitamin or herb said to be good for the brain: Some swear by red wine. One study recommends drinking an alcoholic beverage once a day. Green tea is supposed to be helpful.

An Alzheimer-phobic friend does the word jumble puzzles in the newspaper and practices writing with her left hand. I listen to French language tapes in the car. We are not the only ones who worry. Alzheimer's disease is the second most feared disease of people between the ages of fifty-five and sixty-four, according to the Alzheimer's Association. The first is heart disease. The third is cancer.

But the heartening news is that, when not affected by disease, the aging brain can chug along just fine. Common thinking was once that everybody got a little dingy as they aged, but not so. Research shows that the brain is very plastic and can rebuild itself even into old age. But we have to exercise our brains and feed them well, just like we do for our hearts and arteries.

The Alzheimer's Association reports evidence connecting vascular disease in the brain and what happens to the brain in people with Alzheimer's. The same risk factors for heart attack and stroke also raise the risk of developing dementia. So if we watch our cholesterol and blood pressure, keep our weight down, stop smoking, and start exercising we'll be getting a two-for-one deal. Strong heart, sharp brain.

Brainy women do the following:

- Keep weight, blood pressure, cholesterol, and blood sugar levels within the recommended ranges.

- Eat less fat and more antioxidant-rich foods.

- Move that body. Exercise keeps the blood flowing and may encourage new brain cell growth.

- Push that brain. Read, write your memoirs, play cribbage.

- Get out more. Socializing is good for the brain.

- Be happy. Smiling releases serotonin in the brain.

- Avoid head injuries. Wear your helmet. Use seat belts. Work on balance exercises.

- Don't smoke or drink excessively.

- Drink lots of water. Eat fiber.

- Live fully and for today.

- Knock on wood (my personal favorite).

Time for Your Inner Life

Many a young woman's first act of rebellion, or of simple independence, is to stop attending religious services when she leaves home. We wanted options. We took classes in world religions, visited our friends' more exotic churches and temples, studied goddess worship, decided God had to be a woman, got into Transcendental Meditation, and still feel it's bad luck to tell anyone your mantra. We were open to anything.

Then some of us closed down that part of our lives. There was so much else going on. Marriage, kids, house, job, running for the school board, saving the redwoods. Choosing a spiritual path would have to wait, like cleaning the closets.

But then at some point that old curiosity crept back. Maybe it had to do with turning fifty and considering certain inevitabilities. Or making a life and wondering what it was all about. There began this longing.

Midlife Awakening

Anne Scott, who was raised Episcopalian and later connected with Sufism in her forties, thinks that there is a natural reason for women to explore their spiritual selves at midlife. "I've noticed that women, especially when their children have grown, feel a deep longing for something that they may not even be able to identify. It doesn't get filled by work or partner or home, even though all those aspects of life may be fulfilling in themselves. There seems to be a deeper need and it doesn't go away.

"For some, they will find another pursuit that may temporarily fill this longing, but for others, they come to the realization that they are here for a purpose and they want to know what this is. It is so natural, this awakening; it can appear as depression, or yearning, or feeling the suffering of the world more acutely. Sometimes it may be a desire for silence, or peace, or just a nagging irritation that keeps returning in its own puzzling way."

She thinks it's a universal experience. "There's a global awakening to the qualities of the feminine—the sacredness of life and our interconnectedness as a whole. Women in their midlife seem to be aware of a certain responsibility and are drawn to understanding what this means in their own lives."

Through her DreamWeather Foundation Anne leads dream workshops and helps organize retreats with other women's spirituality groups. In 2002 she participated in an international gathering of five hundred women religious leaders in Geneva, Switzerland, which joined Christians, Muslims, Jews, Hindus, and women of faith from seventy-five countries to create peace-building plans with the United Nations. She's part of Gather the Women, a Web site and group of spiritual women working toward world peace, a combination that some say is the next phase of feminism and political activism.

"This isn't just my California imaginings," says Anne. "Women everywhere want to shift the consciousness to a sense of unity and oneness. If we listen attentively to our inner life we will hear something deeper than the prevailing sound of the world news."

Martha the Methodist from Memphis

Martha Wagley of Memphis does not fit the stereotype of a Methodist minister, or even a person from Tennessee for that matter, at least in style—with her red hair, purple leather gloves, and double ear piercings. In her late fifties she became senior pastor of the First United Methodist Church, a limestone and granite landmark with a clock tower and gold cross in downtown Memphis. There she found "a gracious congregation and a good match for my ability and sense of ministry," and she hopes to serve until she's seventy, the mandatory retirement age for Methodist ministers.

In her thirties, Martha went from being a classic Southern housewife to seminary student, one of three women out of two hundred students. "The administration didn't know what to do with me and I wasn't sure what to do with myself. Every minister was male. The language of clergy was so exclusively male—all the references to 'he' and 'him.'"

Her husband encouraged her, even though both knew Martha was going against Southern tradition. "I had been your very typical Southern wife, raised to look good and to be polite, kind, and gracious. To stay home and take care of the children, prepare meals, and have them ready when your husband comes home. But this model of Southern womanhood started cracking when Mama went back to school and then had to get a job to afford school."

As a Southern white woman in the 1970s, she says, "I knew my place and had a well-defined way of life ahead for me. It was a long shot that I would even be ordained." But she had "a huge, deep sense of call. I knew this is what I had to do."

After five years of school, she was ordained and got her first ministerial position with a small country church. She went on, in the late 1990s, to lead the largest church served by a woman minister in the United Methodist system, the three-thousand-member Germantown church outside of Memphis. "It was unusual for a woman to serve a church with over two thousand. What we call 'high steeple churches' were a real stronghold for men," she says, and her high-profile appointment caused some resistance among parishioners who weren't expecting a woman. Since then she's watched things improve for women clergy. In general, acceptance of women church leaders has grown as more women enter and stay in the ministry for long periods. By 2000 one in every eight American clergy was female.

Speaking before a congregation every Sunday, Martha says, continues to be "thrilling and empowering. For me it's a combination of incredible excitement and fear. There's the mystery of it and the mystical part of trying to proclaim something outside of yourself and beyond."

Martha sees many people at midlife either returning to church or going to church for the first time. Part of that, she believes, is a desire to find community. "The shelves are filled with books on spirituality, but how that connects a person to a church is missing. You can sit in a beautiful setting at the lake and read and pray but what you miss is the connection with community. Spirituality is about me. Church is about you and me and us together. I can sing in a screened porch over the Mississippi River but I don't have the combination of voices that I get in church singing 'Amazing Grace, how sweet the sound.' That's when my heart just lifts."

Being part of a church, she says, "provides the sense that we're not alone. But it's not just that. It's a place to combine our resources for food and clothes and Christmas presents for people. It's where you give service."

Journey to Judaism

Marcia said her meditation teacher once told her she was "allergic" to religion. "I wasn't raised within any religious tradition and I had come to learn meditation strictly as a relaxation technique. I wasn't interested in spiritual discipline and certainly not religious instruction. I was a corporate public relations executive working fifty-plus hours a week handling highly charged media, public, and legislative relations. I just needed to chill out."

So how did she become Jewish? "A funny thing can happen when you calm down," says Marcia, who lives in Northern California. "I found what I didn't know I was looking for, a belief in God as the underlying source of all life. No lightning bolts, visions or voices from on high."

She realized, too, that she longed for religious tradition and to be part of a spiritual community, after observing its importance in others' lives. Then, one day while walking through a used book store, she bent down to straighten a book sticking out from a bottom shelf. The book title was *Sabbath* and it discussed the concept of "sacred rest." That led her to read all she could about Judaism, have many meetings with a rabbi, attend synagogue, and begin the process of becoming Jewish and what she believes will be "a lifetime of study."

She does Shabbat dinners at home, lighting the candles and singing the blessings with her non-Jewish husband and son. She says she still feels challenged by parts of the religion but has come to think of it as she thinks of marriage, "loving someone in spite of their imperfections."

"When you get Jewish, Catholic, Buddhist, Hindu, and Sufi women all practicing their faith in the same room, another religion emerges which is feminine spirituality."
—**carole lee flinders**

RIPE AND RESOLUTE

We've got places to go, friends to make, things to learn, and new goals to meet. What do you promise yourself to finally achieve before your next birthday . . . or decade?

- Learn to meditate.

- Get real about your finances.

- Schedule a day to do nothing.

- Prepare for earthquakes, tornadoes, and other disasters.

- Do a full headstand.

- Complete the Friday *New York Times* crossword puzzle.

- Keep a journal. It will help you when you write your memoir.

- Make up with your daughter-in-law.

- Find a nonprofit that shares your passion and give generously in time and money.

- Read Sartre.

- Give away all shoes that hurt your feet.

- Call the people you've said you wished you had time for and make a date.

- Oh, and don't forget, if you're going to last through the long haul you have to take care of things. Get those darned medical tests. Take your vitamins. Drink your water. Do your Kegels. Make your will. It sets a good example.

PART THREE

A Juicy Legacy

Woman of the Century . . . So Far

Nancy Pelosi became House Democratic leader in 2003, attaining a perch that American women have been moving toward since we won the vote. The first woman to hold a top Congressional leadership post, she became the most powerful woman in Washington DC.

Nancy Pelosi first ran for the U.S. House of Representatives seat when her youngest child was a senior in high school. By then she'd already headed the Democratic Party in California. The petite woman with the flashing smile—taking flak and facing down the president and others on Capitol Hill—became a symbol of what women can be, even though she often said her success has to do with her experience and not her gender.

When she won a Woman of the Year Award from *Ms.* magazine she said, "American life is improved by the involvement of women." But she also said, "I don't want you to vote for me because I'm a woman but I don't want anyone to vote against me because I'm a woman."

Mother of five, grandmother of five, known for being strong on civil liberties and a sucker for Grateful Dead music and chocolate, the House minority leader represents a boon for women, Democrats, and the state of California but is also good PR for the whole country. No

WANTED: MORE WOMEN IN CHARGE

In 2005, women held 15 percent of seats in the U.S. Congress—14 percent of the Senate and 15.2 percent of the House of Representatives.

Women held 25.7 percent of elected executive offices in the nation's fifty state governments, or 81 out of 315 available positions.

In state legislatures, they held 22.5 percent of seats, representing a fourfold increase since 1971.

matter what you think of her politics, no one can deny that this woman speaks volumes for America's diversity. This is what democracy looks like—a pro-choice, Catholic, Italian-American grandmother who is a major player.

Your Country Needs You!

Understanding that "the personal is political" can really start to resonate with women as they get older, says Laurie Young, director of OWL, the Older Women's League, a Washington DC–based organization that advocates for women aged forty and over. Laurie, a fifty-five-year-old mother of an eleven-year-old daughter, says how one gets involved politically usually depends on what's most crucial in your life at the time.

For many years, Laurie cared for both her elderly mother and her young daughter, so she knows about sandwich generation priorities—improved caregiving for elders on one end and child-care options on the other.

What's your issue? Social security, health care reform, Medicare, reproductive rights, cancer research, stem cell studies, domestic abuse, paid family leave, prenatal care? Whatever it is, there's too much at risk to simply be watching when you could be winning.

"There's a cohort of women in their fifties and older who have been politically aware all their lives," says Laurie, "and they continue to be active, maybe even more when they finish raising their kids. I see a lot of women approaching retirement age who are looking for ways to go from political awareness to action."

SOME WAYS TO DO IT

The Internet —"This puts advocacy right at people's fingertips," says Laurie. "It's the fastest way to become an activist. With a few clicks you can send e-mails to your congressional representative."

Visit your person in Congress — They all spend recess time in their district and they all meet with constituents in Washington. It's better than C-Span. Find out up close how the process works.

Run for public office — We need more women candidates who are smart and honorable, with varied experience and fresh solutions. Just be prepared for personal scrutiny and a sometimes bruising campaign. Or work to get someone you care about elected.

Stay informed — Know who represents you, locally, statewide, and nationally. Go to a town meeting or a state convention. Join a civic group whose issues are the same as your own.

Sign up for a women's leadership training program — The White House Project recruits and trains women to run for political office. It also monitors how the media covers women officeholders. You can also find leadership training programs through the YWCA, EMILY'S List, and the National Federation of Republican Women.

"One woman can change the world, but it's easier when you work in groups." **—slogan of the national council of women's organizations**

View from the Top

Lynn Woolsey walked into the House of Representatives at age fifty-five, saw her name among those of the new members, and said, "Oh my God." She says she felt dazzled by her position for "about a week, until I learned that I was nothing compared to a senator and a senator was nothing compared to the president. There's a level of humility all the way along here."

She was elected to the House in 1992, making a big leap from small business owner and city council member. But it was an early domestic hardship, when she was divorced and had to go on public assistance to raise four children, that gave her the bootstrap clout that goes along with being the first former single mother on welfare to serve in Congress.

"I know I have one of the most powerful jobs in the world and every single day I remind myself that this is happening on my watch. I tell myself, 'Okay, Woolsey, what can you do about it?'" She said it took a few reelections to Congress for her to realize that she "had the mandate to go ahead and speak out."

She's done so, against the war in Iraq, for paid family leave, against privatizing Social Security, for protecting the coast and maintaining other environmental safeguards. Sometimes she pushes legislation just to get the discussion going. She introduced a bill that would require paid family leave, allowing parents to care for new babies, attend school events, and deal with family emergencies; increase child-care programs; and provide financial incentives to recruit better-qualified child-care workers and provide free preschool for all children.

At the time she told a reporter that she knew the bill had no chance of passing into law but that she thought legislators needed to be talking about it "so that someday people will pay attention." She's proud of being called "the conscience of the Congress" by her colleague

Nancy Pelosi for taking unpopular stands. "I'm clear on my convictions," she says. "I have a brave heart."

The *Washington Post* once pointed out her gutsy position on gray hair, saying that Lynn is one of those rare Washington women not to color her tresses. She says she's too busy to color it, but she also enjoys the novelty. "When I got divorced somebody bet me I would color my hair and get cosmetic surgery. I said I bet you a thousand bucks I won't." Gray hair is not a professional drawback in a job that has no term limits or age limits, says Lynn. Sexism, she says, is more of an issue than ageism in DC. In the 109th Congress, the average age of women senators, representatives, and delegates was fifty-six and a half.

"There are also a lot of old men running around Washington." And, in general, it is a place where seniority matters. "What counts is wisdom and experience. The highest-ranking people in Congress are the ones with experience."

She says she's never had a mentor but counts on her adult daughter to give her honest advice. "She's a lot like me, only better. I feel pretty certain that she watched me when she was growing up and thought she could do what I do, but in a smoother way. She's absolutely clear when she thinks I'm off track."

Lynn does have several role models, including the late congresswoman Patsy Mink from Hawaii, who was

TOMATOES AT THE TOP

Gutsy, outspoken government leaders making a difference who even if you don't agree with politically you'd love to meet for lunch.

- Sen. Barbara Boxer
- Sen. Hillary Clinton
- Sen. Susan Collins
- Elizabeth Dole
- Sen. Dianne Feinstein
- Gov. Christine Gregoire
- Rep. Barbara Lee
- Sen. Lisa Murkowski
- Gov. Janet Napolitano
- Rep. Nancy Pelosi
- Condoleezza Rice
- Rep. Ileana Ros-Lehtinen
- Rep. Jan Schakowsky
- Sen. Olympia Snowe
- Rep. Lynne Woolsey

instrumental in establishing Title IX, a law that guaranteed full participation for young women in sports and education. "Patsy had the littlest body and this very big voice. They kept stomping on her but she took it."

She's learned from others, including Nancy Pelosi, Maxine Waters, and Pat Schroeder, all of whom were elected to Congress before Lynn got there. "I learned about generosity and graciousness from Nancy, and the importance of supporting people who are not in as powerful a position as yourself. From Maxine I learned to be fearless and not worry about retribution. From Pat, I learned to focus on the issues that are most important to you and not be all over the map."

With women still the minority in Congress, Lynn says there are certain things that they have to worry about that men don't. For example, there's the importance of voice. "Women's voices are not as easy to listen to as men. It's the sound. If we get shrill or start to sound bossy or nagging, people quit listening. You have to be aware of your delivery."

Lynn came up with a plan to have the Democratic women in the House stand and line up in the aisle during crucial floor votes in solidarity over particular issues. "Maybe it's on Social Security, Medicare, or prescription drugs, something that we want to show we're behind because of how it will affect women. It makes such a statement with us all there in our brightest suits. I think it scares the bejesus out of the men, on both sides of the aisle."

She's learned to be thick-skinned in the face of criticism, but when a reporter described a challenger to her seat in Congress as being younger and more energetic, Lynn took offense. Younger in years, she conceded, but no one, she says, surpasses her energy. "Passion and energy, that's who I am. I've always been told that since I was a kid."

"Once, power was considered a masculine attribute. In fact, power has no sex." —katharine graham, publisher

Sexual Politics and Golf

Martha Burk is one of those Texas women in the mold of Ann Richards, Molly Ivins, and Lady Bird Johnson. Good old girls, some call them—independent, intelligent, spirited, humorous, gracious, and with a disarming charm that can skewer opponents so slyly that they don't even realize they're bleeding.

She's a former Dallas housewife with a Ph.D. in political psychology who, when she went looking for a university faculty job, was asked to take a typing test. By the time she hit middle age she had become one of the leading spokeswomen for gender equality. When she hit sixty she was not only a media star but a media survivor as well.

As director of the National Council of Women's Organizations (NCWO), she runs the nation's oldest coalition of women's groups—two hundred organizations including the Feminist Majority, Hadassah, NOW, and the YWCA. Martha has long spoken about issues that matter to women and contributed commentary to national publications. But her name and face didn't become widely familiar, and despised by some, until she took on the men-only rule at the Augusta Golf Club, home of the Masters Tournament.

On behalf of the NCWO she wrote a note to the chairman of the Augusta National Golf Club in 2002, urging him to open membership to women. Martha says she was surprised when the issue grew from "what I thought would be a one-day story to a media tsunami." Her challenge drew the indignation of misogynists, rednecks, and corporate big boys around the country, who protested in everything from clipped business tones to smarmy personal attacks, basically saying, "You bitches want to destroy the country."

"A man approached me in New York City, asked if I was Martha Burk, and pointed his finger in my face and said, 'Let me tell you . . .' I stopped him and said, 'If I were a man you wouldn't be sticking a finger in my face.'"

Regarding Augusta, she says, "I have nothing against women's poker groups and men's sewing circles, but you can use privacy only to a point, and not when you use it as a means to discriminate. This was a private club acting as a public entity. Their answer was, it's tradition, the word that has been used so often to enforce discrimination. It was never about golf. It's about women and what we're allowed to do."

The Augusta club member roster included "people who control companies larger than some countries. They stood together. They said gender discrimination is okay, no big deal."

Martha says she's become braver as she's grown older. "I have been the target of very high-profile criticism due to my work in the women's rights movement. The key is realizing that it goes with the job and not to take it personally, though some of the attacks have been vicious and personal. Augusta took me to a whole new level of name and face recognition. It's been worth it to get some coverage for women's issues in general. I think as you get older your values change; you care less about appearances and more about getting things done or making change."

For others who want to get things done but may be concerned about the mudslinging side of politics, Martha advises, "Don't take it personally. Never get down on their level. Smile a lot and take the high road."

"The rooster crows but the hen delivers."
—ann richards

Mother Nature's Broads

Legend has it that a group of women hikers were in Utah to celebrate the anniversary of the Wilderness Act around the same time Senator Orrin Hatch made a pronouncement that wilderness areas were not accessible to older people and, therefore, more roads were needed to allow the elderly to get in to use the land.

Oh, moose-honky, said the hikers, coming in from one of their wilderness hikes. As one got up to go to the bathroom, another hiker looked at her admiringly and said, "Now, there goes a great old broad."

And so was born the Great Old Broads for Wilderness, dedicated to the belief that what is needed is more wilderness, not more roads. Based in Durango, Colorado, the Great Old Broads consider themselves "not just a hiking group, but a hiking group with a purpose," says Ronni Egan, executive director. These women share a concern for what humans are doing to the Earth and a desire to leave a legacy of healthy lands. Their aim is to expand the wilderness and protect it from road building, because "once there's a road into a place it's no longer a wilderness."

Other threats to the wilderness are off-road vehicles, oil and gas leases, and sloppy campers who abuse fragile environments. One Broads project in the southwestern United States is to monitor dirt bikes, snowmobiles, and off-road vehicles and their damaging effects and to share their reports with land management agencies, conservationists, attorneys, and the media. In addition, they lobby Washington legislators regarding various threats to wilderness areas, write letters, stage protests, and in general "raise a ruckus," while getting out in the wilds as much as possible.

At last count, there were twenty-six hundred Great Old Broads, representing every state and ranging in age from thirties to nineties. The majority are middle aged and older. Younger ones are called "Broads-in-Training." Men are welcome, too. Ronni says all Broads "have energy and passion and are willing to sink their teeth into things." And they do it in hiking boots and bad hair, without worrying about broken fingernails.

Their name and high visibility make them a media curiosity, and their maturity earns them respect. They've lived long enough to have a perspective on waste, to know how easily nature can be ruined and how hard it is to resurrect. Members have rallied in large numbers to support environmental protection in places from Vermont to the Arctic National Wildlife Refuge.

At Yellowstone National Park the Broads joined a long-running controversy about snowmobiles. "Here were all these cross-country skiers in their Lycra," says Ronni, "and the press zeroed in on us in our snowshoes, gas masks, and animal costumes."

Ronni seems born to be a Broad. She grew up riding horses and living away from people in the sparsely populated Southwest. In college she studied animal husbandry, art, and philosophy and went on to work as an outfitter and guide on guest ranches in New Mexico and Colorado.

"I feel that I can be more fully who I am out in the river, climbing on the rocks. No one is judging me. It doesn't matter what I look like, what church I go to, or what books I read. It's all a matter of what I can physically do and it simplifies everything. I always tell people that the wilderness is my shrink, my church, and my health club."

Women and Mother Nature, she says, are a natural fit. "I think that women are uniquely suited to seeing things in a holistic, more than a linear, sense. The environmental activist world has to do with nurturing, not controlling." Speaking for herself, Ronni says being in the wilderness makes a person appreciate "the continuum of time, the value of long life, the cyclical nature of things. You get out there and you know you won't be here forever and there will be things replacing you.

"I think where society is going radically astray is to think that technology will fix everything. We need to recognize we're an integral part of the big system. If one piece isn't healthy, all is not healthy. Trees, cockroaches, we're all in this together."

HOW NOT TO BE AN OLD POOP

Attitude may not be everything, but it's certainly as important as a good colorist, if you don't want to get stuck in that over-the-hill stereotype. Here are some ways to act your age in a good way and set a positive example for those who are watching and taking notes.

1. **Be yourself.** Know who you are and don't worry about those who automatically judge you for being of a certain vintage.

2. **Be confident.** Strive for "total confidence," says Alison, a college professor and author who learned from an elegant and clever mother. "No more 'Do I look okay?' or 'Should I *really*?' You know you're okay."

3. **Be witty.** Maintain a sense of humor, the type of humor that is seasoned, knowing, and comes from years of grand insights about the absurdities of life.

4. **Be wise . . . but don't lecture.** Cultivate "a quiet knowing," says Alison. "You don't have to say it but if someone asks, you may offer a few kernels of wisdom without the overbearing 'You know what you need to do.'"

5. **Be a listener.** You listen because you have the time or you make the time. You can still learn from others.

6. **Be generous.** Resist being jealous of those who have what you want, especially the person twenty-five years younger whose last book advance would have paid off your mortgage. Better to follow the Buddhist idea of sympathetic joy for someone else's accomplishment.

Rebels Without a Stitch

Donna Sheehan lives in an old boat barn on Northern California's Tomales Bay, right along the San Andreas Fault, from which she started her own earth-shaking movement in 2002. Donna, an artist, convinced her friends and neighbors in Marin

County to take off their clothes, lie down in a wet soccer field, and curl their nude bodies to spell out the word *peace* for a photographer. It was a last-ditch effort to get the attention of the mainstream media, which at the time seemed to be ignoring all peace protests. One woman compared their effort to that of "the gentleman who stood that day in Tiananmen Square. It makes me feel that we could stop a war."

Donna called her creation "Baring Witness" and defined the event as an installation instead of an action, but the silent tableau she believes effectively helped communicate to people outside the United States that not all Americans wanted a war.

They didn't stop the United States from going to war but they did get attention and Donna continued to set up more installations throughout California, sometimes with the peace sign or the words *No More War*. Soon the BBC was visiting Donna's house, and copycat groups around the country and the world, inspired by Donna's, started going stark naked for peace, from Japan to Minnesota. A Baring Witness calendar, book, and documentary followed. At one count there were two hundred reenactments around the world and not all for antiwar efforts. Nude women in India protested police brutality outside a police station where abuses occurred.

A longtime environmentalist, Donna had never participated in a peace demonstration. "None of us are exhibitionists," says Donna, who is in her seventies and normally favors jeans and a turtleneck. "We're all self-conscious about our lumps and bumps and felt extremely vulnerable. But I think every woman felt empowered after we did it."

There's precedent. In the eleventh century, Lady Godiva rode in the buff through an English market to demand lower taxes on behalf of the poor. In 2001, Nigerian women took over an oil refinery owned by Chevron/Texaco and threatened to disrobe if improvements weren't made in their village. Their daring action was even more controversial because of the fact that a woman revealing her nakedness is considered a shaming gesture in the Nigerian tribal culture. Donna says nude protests will be effective as long as nudity gets people's attention. "At any time or place, any woman might expose all for peace and justice. Her only intent is to seduce men into listening."

A Berkeley woman who had joined a Baring Witness group of ninety naked women on a Pacific beach creating the message "No More War" said it was the culmination of a lifetime of pacifism, which began when she saw pictures of the devastation in Hiroshima while still in high school. Lying still on wet sand was not good for her arthritic knee, she said, but "ninety women without a stitch on made people sit up and take notice."

NOT YOUR MOTHER'S STYLE OF PROTEST

Anthropologist Margaret Mead wrote, "Never doubt that a small group of thoughtful, comitted people can change the world; indeed it's the only thing that ever has." Margaret also coined the term "post-menopausal zest." Imagine what small dedicated groups of zesty post-menopausal women can do.

"Women may be the one group that grows more radical with age."
—gloria steinem

WHAT TO DO ABOUT THE FOLKS?

Nearly two-thirds of Americans under age sixty expect to be responsible for the care of an elderly relative in the next ten years, according to the National Partnership for Women and Families. How do we decide how to do that?

- Understand your rights about taking time off under the Family and Medical Leave Act.

- How long can you afford to be off work?

- What does your parent or family member need from you? Dropping groceries by and driving to doctor's appointments? Or full-time move-in care?

- Can they live with you? Is there room in your home?

- Can you hire a caregiver to come in when you're at work?

They Took Care of Us

"When I met my husband ten years ago, I told him that I would go back to Missouri to take care of my mom and dad when they needed it," says Linda, a former flight attendant who now travels a regular path between her house in California and her parents' in Missouri. She's not alone.

"I know so many people my age running back and forth to their parents' home or bringing them to their home to care for them," says Linda. Her sixty years puts her at the oldest end of the boomer bulge; her parents, in their eighties, are in the fastest-growing and neediest segment of the American population.

Linda goes to Missouri for weeks at a time to stay with her parents in the house and town that have been their life. "I want to keep them in their house as long as I can. My dad is eighty-seven and my mom's eighty-four. He's aging faster. He has to use a walker and he's lost some of his faculties. But he's still wise.

"My mother has anxiety problems and needs moral support. She worries a lot. When I'm here it calms her. Both of my parents have been such hard workers. It must be hard to face that you can't do things for yourself. At my age I have aches and pains but I'm nowhere near where they are."

Truth be told, we're all getting there. The swell of aging boomers is already a concern of government and service providers, from Medicare to senior centers. But before we become the old folks, we have our parents to care for.

Like Linda, we think about what they did for us, and now it's our turn to help them out. Linda basically runs the house for her parents. "I do the cooking, cleaning, and laundry. I take my mother to the grocery store and to her hair appointments. My brother lives next door but he's a farmer and very busy. My parents were farmers too. Soybeans and corn. It's amazing to think of all the changes my father has seen in farming. He used to do it all by hand with horses, checking the corn by hand, not in a heated, ventilated cab.

"I don't want my father to ever go into a home. He'd just die. I know there will be a time when we can't take care of him. He needs help getting dressed and my mother can do that now. But he's a big man and we'll need to find some paid help to come in when he gets worse. I'll do it as long as I can."

Mollie is dealing with similar issues. One day, long after her stroke, Mollie's mother said, "We didn't really get along, did we?" Mollie recalls answering, "You don't have to think about that now because it's not happening anymore."

By then Mollie and her husband had driven to Seattle, collected her mother and her belongings, and brought her back with them to Northern California. "The last couple of

- What does your parent want to do?
- What does his/her insurance cover in terms of home care?
- Is there respite care available so you can get a break?
- Is an assisted living residence an option?
- Most important of all, who can advise?

Here are a few sources:

- The National Alliance for Caregiving **www.caregiving.org**
- National Association of Area Agencies on Aging **www.n4a.org**
- The National Council on Aging **www.ncoa.org**
- National Long Term Care Ombudsman Resource Center **www.ltcombudsman.org**

miles driving here she got very quiet. I tried to explain that she would be living near us," says Mollie. "I told her that she couldn't go back to Seattle, not now."

What to do about mom and dad isn't something a lot of people plan for. Some have an idea of what their parents would like if they became incapacitated. Mollie knew that her parents had made a living will before her father died. But she and her mother hadn't spoken for four years when a family friend in Seattle called to say her seventy-nine-year-old mother had suffered a stroke. It fell to Mollie to make all the decisions because she was the only living relative.

"I have to admit that I thought, wait a minute. Here's a woman who disliked us so much she didn't talk to us for years. Now I have to take care of her." Nevertheless, she found her mother a room in an assisted living home that cost $3,000 a month, which Mollie felt was affordable considering her mother had investments and savings. "But then I got worried because the stock market took a dive and we're not very smart about money. I had to rely on her stockbroker in Seattle, who said to hang on. I felt I had no choice but to take his advice, but I would wake up in the middle of the night panicked about what to do if she ran out of money. We lived in a one-bedroom house. Where would we put her? Even if she did live with us, we both work every day and how could we afford to have someone come in?"

But the money lasted, and Mollie's mother died four years later. Something sweet happened in that time. "She became kinder. I felt sorry for her having the stroke and losing so much of her memory, but it seemed to put her in a gentler, simpler place. She used to be so judgmental and stubborn. She became nice." She even warmed up to Mollie's husband, whom she'd never liked, and he to her. "Wes was incredible with my mother and before she got sick she had been shitty to him, but he put all that aside to make her life a wee bit more fun."

"Imitate the trees. Learn to lose in order to recover, and remember that nothing stays the same for long, not even pain, psychic pain. Sit it out. Let it all pass. Let it go." —**may sarton**

Payback Time

Gloria Steinem once told Judy Collins that you can tell everything about a person if you look in their checkbook and see what they give money to and the causes they support. At some point, maybe when we're doing our wills, or at tax time, we all start to consider what charities we sponsor, whether it's the firehouse pancake breakfast and the Save the Egret jar at the grocery store, the annual pledge drive for public radio, or the auction item for the women's justice center fund-raiser.

Tracy Gary, in her book *Inspired Philanthropy,* reports it's not just the wealthy who give. In fact, she says, the bulk of financial support for nonprofits comes from households with incomes of less than $60,000. Americans are generous. Giving went way up following the 9/11 attacks. And compared to most of the world's population, we're all wealthy. According to the U.S. Census Bureau, if you earn any money at all you have more money than 1 billion people in the world.

But say you suddenly had more money to give—how would you choose? Jane, who lives in the Midwest, inherited great wealth from her parents, who had a lucrative family business. She won't say how much, beyond "a ton." Her big challenge was not figuring out how often to go to Europe or where to buy another house, but whom to help.

"I don't think of this money I inherited as my money. I have my own money that I earned, and I give a part of that away and always have. But the way I look at my parents' money is that it really belongs to the community. This is the community that helped my parents earn the money and a place that has treated me well. So I think I owe it back."

In addition to writing out checks, Jane, who gave up her full-time editing job after her parents died, now gives more hours to community efforts than she could afford to before. Again, she has to make a choice.

"I have former colleagues who can't believe I go to so many meetings now, but I only go to ones that I want to. I quit one board because I felt frustrated and like I was wasting my time. There was bad leadership and I couldn't get anything done about it. I find I'm pretty good at it, being on a board. It's amazing, the nonprofits who don't have much business sense or sensibility. I find that I actually know stuff and can offer good advice.

"The one thing I've done is not say yes just to say yes, and be on every board in town." It's not surprising that she gets asked a lot, because of her family name, but also because she is well known in the city where she's lived most of her life. "A friend of my mother's invited me to lunch with the guy who runs the opera. I told her, 'I hate the opera. I don't get it and I am tone deaf.' I would be glad to have lunch, but I felt I had to be up front."

An art history major in college, Jane prefers to put both time and money into the local art museums and an art school. She also serves on the boards of two colleges, a hospital foundation, a women's fund, a neighborhood community center, and a community foundation. She also raises funds for a professional organization.

Because of conflicts of interest she doesn't contribute to any political campaigns. Instead, she has always given to her church. "It's something we were taught to do, to tithe to the church and, as we grew older, to other worthwhile places. I started tithing before I could really afford it. I always had a membership to the art museum at a fairly high level because I've always loved art. I learned from my father about giving. He used to send a giant check every so often to his alma mater, not at a regular gift-giving time and for no apparent reason. He'd tell the university president to use it however he thought best."

When her father died the family ended up with "money way beyond what we needed. He really left it so that my brother and sister and I had to decide what to do. I kind of got even with him in a cool way by plastering his name all over buildings and school programs, which he might have hated but seems so appropriate. It's very rewarding to have given something to his alma mater with his name on it that now funds a great speaker series."

Jane and her siblings also put their parents' names on a new addition to the art museum where their mother had been a docent and their father had served on the board. "It's in honor of Mom and Daddy from us," she says.

She contributes to the city zoo because, she says, "I believe in what they do, particularly now that it is much more conservation driven. I do think there is a chance we can save the world, however Pollyanna-ish that sounds. Plus, our love for animals came from our parents." Jane also devotes weekend hours to working in the zoo gardens. "I'm the day laborer. I weed and slash dead bulb leaves, get covered in dirt, and scare the poop out of the la-di-da types who come by and recognize me. It keeps me humble."

Time or Money

Have you always given through payroll deduction to your company's United Way campaign, or do you wait until the veteran's group calls to sell you light bulbs and garbage bags? Do you still feel like you're surrounded by people with their hands out? You're not alone. In the United States there are 1.6 million nonprofits, and to keep afloat, they depend more on the little people than on big corporations.

But you're just a poor working woman, you say. There's not much left over to donate. However, there are other ways to help your favorite cause. You can join the board. Help put on a fund-raiser. Sell lavender in front of the grocery store to raise money to help troubled kids. Convince your artist friends to donate a piece for the auction to help people with AIDS.

As for what you leave behind—money for a music camp for kids or for the woman who rescues feral cats—you probably want to make sure the charity does what it says it will when they get the big check from your estate.

Who Comes After You?

"It's the sizzle," says Barbara Branic about mentoring, "to make myself available to high-potential people who really want me to help them." The Indiana bank president considers mentoring an obligation. "I do it because I benefited from people (mostly males) who got out of their comfort zone to help me, to say, 'You didn't approach that very well.' Or to call after a meeting and say, 'I'm so proud of you for asking that question.'

"I try to be very intentional, mentoring the staff that reports to me directly," says the bank president, "to ask them, what is the one thing they would like to do better and to know more about in the next year? The idea is to discuss how to make things better, not just to complain. But it's okay to put the ugly stuff out on the table. And I make sure they know there are no stupid questions."

Rather than formally offering herself as a mentor, she will hand select a person who has potential, "someone I don't want to lose to the competition. I let them know I want to know more about them. I ask them to lunch, ask what they want to do next and go from there."

"Mentoring is not about passing on power," says Ellen Boneparth, whose career as an educator, writer, and policy maker has focused on global women's issues. She says that mentoring for her has a lot to do with never having children "but still having an impact on the next generation."

"Surround yourself by people smarter than you," advises Billie Blair, who runs a community foundation in Santa Fe. The way she mentors younger women is to "convey the vision and give them their head. I tell them to know men's rules because we're still going to be playing by them for a while. And love 'em [men]. Don't diss 'em. As my mother always said, you catch more flies with honey than with vinegar."

I'll Be There

Shermane grew up on Motown and spent her first allowance on Dionne Warwick's "Walk on By." Now the fifty-one-year-old lawyer goes to Eminem and 50 Cent concerts with the high school girls she mentors through the same Detroit club she belonged to as a kid.

It's where Shermane learned some of the same lessons about life she now passes on. "You know. The ones that say: Be your own person. Live up to your word. Follow your dream as long as there's some place for you to sleep when you get there.

"Those high school years can be a struggle for mothers and daughters. But a young girl can have a good relationship, find a comfort level, with another adult, and tell someone else things she wouldn't talk about to her parents. I let them talk, and then I give them my full opinion. We talk about schoolwork and careers. I give them advice about different colleges. I tell them if I think a guy is not good for them."

One of her girls went on to Shermane's alma mater, Howard University, and became a TV news anchor. "I'm so proud of her. She calls me 'mom.'" Shermane's own daughter is a lawyer living in Los Angeles, so Shermane looks at mentoring as a way to continue to keep in touch with young minds. "I like to know what's going on with their generation. Some of their stories give me nightmares but it makes me feel good that these young kids want to talk to me."

Her professional focus has recently been on poverty law, but Shermane has a background in entertainment law, which gives her entrée into the Detroit music scene. "Some of my girls work with me on concerts. I show them how to work the soundboard. We discuss the music. I tell them about jazz. They tell me about rap, which I don't really like, but at least I know what it is."

Now Shermane is rethinking her own future. She may go back into the entertainment field, which would require her to relocate. "It's scary to think about, but I'm always telling the girls they should pursue their passion, take a few calculated risks. It makes me think I should, too."

Anti-Sedentary Movement

Georgia O'Keeffe moved in 1949 to her summer place in New Mexico at age sixty-two, swapping the skyscrapers of Manhattan for desert scrub, juniper trees, and big rocks, and, back then, a drive of many hours to Santa Fe.

Nuala O'Faolain, who goes back and forth from her native Ireland to New York, writes about moving to new places in her book *Almost There*. She says, "Intrepid explorers often come from a socially privileged background: the rest of us have to learn how to make our way in strange places step by nervous step."

Yet for many that nervous step is worth it, so that the big change that happens for women after fifty often puts them in a brand-new environment. Former flower child Salli moved to Florida for her husband's business, shocking her friends who couldn't imagine this classic California hippie living in such a foreign spot. At a farewell lunch a friend told Salli that if she didn't like Florida she could move back, although, given the price of Northern California real estate, it's a common understanding that once you sell you don't buy back in. Salli said, "Oh, I'll like it."

It's an adventure, she says, along with a good business move, and she explains that she wasn't always a Californian, having actually been born in Florida and raised in Ohio. And now she gets to swim nude, because she has a pool surrounded by a tall hedge and it's eighty-five degrees in the morning, "which Floridians tell me is not really warm."

Salli's a real "bloom where you are planted" kind of person, but she admits that at times she feels like she's in an alien space. "Michael and I were playing pool one day in the community center near our house, and this woman burst in looking for her husband, saw me, and stopped dead in her tracks. 'A woman?' she bellowed. 'I have never seen a woman in this room before now.' I stood there groping for a smile, hanging onto my pool cue." Yet her neighbors have been very welcoming to them and their wildly painted ceramic pig planted in the front yard.

Caitlin and her husband moved to France to restore an old farmhouse and barn and open a bed-and-breakfast in the Dordogne region. She's the language, wine, and food expert. He's the restoration specialist. They've learned to do business the French way—before noon and after two. They're within bicycle distance of the bakery and international newsstand. Cait stays in touch with their adult children and her parents by e-mail. But sometimes she gets homesick, especially when she hears Joni Mitchell sing "California."

But then, California keeps coming to them. The first summer they were open, they hosted a French wine and food class run by a California chef. They met a couple in the next village who had moved to France from Santa Cruz and told Caitlin where to find a yoga class.

Middle age used to be considered a rather stagnant time in life, a time to reflect, build your equity, and stay put. Now, for many, the smart move is to take the equity and run. The nest is empty, so let's move to another tree. It's like those SUV ads depicting the middle-aged couple who cry, "Yippee!" when the last kid leaves for college and they can now hit the open road.

Gretchen and her husband moved to the Olympic Peninsula on a whim. One Christmas the couple rented a motor home, piled in with their cats, and drove from California to the arty, old seaport town of Port Townsend, Washington. Their goal was just to look around. But they went wild for the region and spent a couple of rainy days looking at property with a realtor. They bought a house, intending to rent it out until they retired in another five years. Within a year they had upped their deadline, quit their jobs (as teacher and plumber), and made the leap. They now have panoramic views of mountains and water, a hot tub facing the forest, a sailboat moored at a nearby marina, and room for kids and grandkids when they come to visit.

"What's most satisfying is starting a new adventure, meeting people, living in a new town, and having the guts to do it," says Gretchen.

Midlife-Friendly Towns

A Los Angeles woman of middle years once explained to me that there are two different LAs—the one she avoids, because she's slightly overweight, has gray hair, and drives an economy car, and the one she prefers because it has more museums and classrooms than bars and clubs.

No, she said, to Melrose Avenue and certain shopping areas in the Hollywood vicinity. Too much of generational divide, she said, with extreme emphasis on clothes and hair. Yes, she said, to the San Gabriel area and Pasadena, which she described as down-to-earth with a healthy age mix. She never would go into a Starbucks in Santa Monica unless she dressed for it. But move a few blocks to the east and she would feel fine most places in a T-shirt and shorts.

A few hundred miles north you'll hear Northern Californians brag that their half of the state puts more emphasis on a person's interior while Southern California cares only for the exterior. A San Francisco writer once said her city is a comfortable spot for middle-aged women because gay men will go right on being nice to you even when your face starts to slide.

IS YOUR TOWN MIDLIFE FRIENDLY?

Some places are just naturally midlife friendly, and others make you feel like you're unwelcome, redundant, and what are you doing in my boutique, old person? Here are some ways to tell if you want to stick around:

1. Do you see many women your age at the theater, jazz clubs, and coffeehouses?

2. Is there a spandex-only rule at the gym?

3. How many Steel Magnolias in town? Got any vintage women judges, rabbis, mayors, newscasters, professors, chefs, cabaret singers? Who's running the nonprofits and the city council?

4. Would the hippest boutique in town let you in the door without your daughter?

5. What's the average age of the downtown workforce?

6. What's the mix on the tennis court, golf courses, and hiking trails?

7. Are people more into liposuction or SPF 45 sunscreen?

8. Is there any place to go for a late-night drink other than a bar named Hooters?

9. Is there anyone else in your night class who can sing along to "R-E-S-P-E-C-T"?

10. Are aging hippies considered eccentrics or vagrants?

11. Would you feel welcome in the hot new restaurant at a table for one?

"If you want to live a long, long time, get involved."
—**molly mcgregor,** director of the national women's history project

PICK YOUR SPOT

Talking about where to move next is as much fun as looking at ads for Bali in February. A number of Web sites can help you match a new town with your climatic, economic, and cultural needs. Just type "compare cities" into a search engine and you'll get a number of sites, like **www.bestplaces.net** and **www.findyourspot.com**. Type in your town and a possible dream town and you'll get comparisons of real estate properties, number of sunny days, caliber of museums, the quantity of Thai restaurants.

Depending on your personal leanings, here are some amenities you might want to consider:

- Proximity to a university
- Quality of public transportation
- Proximity to a major airport
- Leash laws and dog parks

How Friendly Are Your Natives?

Leisa in Houston says her town welcomes all ages and all women who understand that "Texan women run the world. We've got so much room here [that] everybody feels they have a place." Eve favors Boston because it has "a critical mass of politically engaged people of all ages." Gretchen in Chicago says women there are a little chubbier than in California but are comfortable with it. The weather prohibits showing much flesh. "No need to spend thousands having your spider veins removed."

Mary agrees. "The Midwest is great for older, heavier women and Detroit is even better than Chicago. I work in a predominantly black office and some of the heavy black women feel pretty good about themselves. They know they have power and status."

Carole calls Santa Fe "the perfect town for older, free-spirited women who will not be ignored." Jane enjoys Phoenix for the "don't-fence-me-in attitude. There are no rules about being a certain way at a certain age." Emmie moved to a condo in Denver where her neighbors include a young pilot, a Japanese couple, a professional gay man, and a retired female banker from Manhattan. "A good party mix."

Find Your Landscape

A
nn lives in a blue house with white shutters perched on a bluff in one of the most dramatic parts of the Pacific Northwest. Though she lives comfortably on a pension and investments, she chooses to dwell in a small house because, she says, "I don't want to spend all my time cleaning." It's roomy enough for her cat, her crafts, a crystal chandelier in the living room, and her collection of miniature lighthouses.

The woman fits her landscape. Ann's a sturdy can-do woman with rose-colored fingernails who worked almost thirty years as a torpedo mechanic. "I know," she says, anticipating the question. "Most people don't realize that the Navy still makes torpedoes," explaining that her job was to test fire and rebuild the big guns at a Navy installation in another part of Washington. "People say 'Oh, you made weapons that killed people.' Well, not really, because most wars are on land now. The last torpedo fired in anger was in 1944."

The work suited her. "It was fun. I need to do hands-on things, no sitting behind a desk pushing things around." She was only forty-eight when she retired, around the same time her father, and then her stepmother, died. "I retired very unexpectedly and prematurely, almost seven years away from a normal retirement. I hadn't really planned what I would do

- Number of churches
- Number of gyms
- Accessibility of bike and hiking trails
- Number of coffeehouses with outside seating
- Ethnic, political, and economic diversity

But you still have to personally scope the place for those niceties that would make it your kind of town. Visiting Port Townsend, Gretchen took it as a good sign that the women next to her in the movie theater left their purses on their seats when they went to the ladies' room. And that the jazz bar doesn't charge a cover in the winter.

207

after I retired. I think I expected to move closer to my parents. But they died, and I scrapped that plan. I felt like there was no one who really cared what I did, so I said, 'I'm moving.'"

She went a long way, to the opposite end of the country, to a small town in Maine. She bought a house and started working at a lighthouse museum. After making some bad business moves with a new friend who turned out untrustworthy, she moved back to Washington and, like Gretchen and her husband, chose the Victorian seaport town of Port Townsend. "I don't know why I ever thought I could live anywhere but the Pacific Northwest."

Ann, in her mid-fifties, spends her time sailing, volunteering, traveling, and building things. She built her house herself, doing most of the construction, wiring, and insulation while living in a trailer over a long, wet nine months. "Amazing, huh? That a girl could build this."

Sailing is her therapy and main recreation, and she does it in a boat that's big enough to take her to Canada and around the San Juan Islands when she chooses. "You shut your engine off and let the winds carry you along. It's very soothing." When the weather gets fierce she cranks up her gas fireplace at home and works on blankets for Project Linus, a program that distributes new, handmade blankets to ill and traumatized children.

On other rainy days she heads to a nearby marina where boaters get together and do projects in the woodworking shop. "I call it the boys' club. I'm the only woman."

Ann's been married and divorced. "I got along better with a torpedo."

Nevertheless, when she moved to Port Townsend she was worried about how to meet people. "I'm shy and that makes it hard to make friends." The boys' club welcomed her as soon as they learned she could repair docks and solve electrical problems. "I belong to the girls' club, too," she says, adding that she helped organize a chapter of the Red Hat Society in Port Townsend.

Her next goal is to outfit an RV for winter traveling. The Northwest, she says, builds hardy women. "I read the obituaries in the newspaper. A lot of these women last to their eighties and nineties."

Follows Man, Finds Self

Deborah moved to Spain feeling like a "fallen feminist" because she did so more to follow her husband's dream than her own. In San Diego she was the founder and director of a children's theater program, and her husband, Bob, was a college instructor. After a while, he decided he was ready to move to the island of Mallorca, build stone walls, play his trumpet, sit in the village square, and slacken the pace. She wasn't so sure.

They started as summer people, buying a partially completed stone house in a tiny agricultural village in the center of the island. It was a few summers before they began to feel accepted by the townspeople as regulars rather than as tourists. They finished the house, cut the cord to San Diego, and moved to Mallorca permanently. Eventually Deborah could report, "I've fallen in love with our new home, slowly over many years. I love the sense of discovery, new places, and new understandings of what motivates people here. Even if I found myself suddenly on my own, I might very well stay on. So perhaps now I can claim to have chosen a future in a new country."

The town square is a primary gathering spot, where on hot nights the bar turns its TV toward the patio so people can watch TV while they drink beer and eat ice cream. Deborah says most of the villagers are over age sixty-five, "so we are in fact younger than the mean, quite a contrast from Southern California, where old folks are invisible."

Perfecting the language is a constant challenge, even though both have a good working knowledge of Spanish. "Sometimes it feels like you're under water or you have a filter obscuring your ability to perceive that can be both amusing or alarming," says Deborah. "Or suddenly I'll understand something outside of my usual perception. But it's cool to be challenged by what was so underappreciated formerly, the ability to communicate in your native language. In some sense, living here is like going back in time. We see couples returning from their fields on little carts and it's not unusual to have to stop your car as several women finish up a conversation in the middle of the street."

Having taken a course in teaching English as a second language before leaving San Diego, and drawing on her theater skills, Deborah started teaching a class that combines improvisational acting with English lessons. They have Spanish friends and other expat friends, including American couples they met working on the Americans Overseas for Kerry campaign. "We've managed some wonderful parties where Spanish, French, and English was heard around the table. I feel we've become part of an outpost, sharing political views and the luxury of free time and the desire to enjoy it. It feels like a second adolescence, replete with hormonal challenges."

Now, to See the Rest of the World

In her book *Gutsy Women,* full of travel tips for women, Marybeth Bond quotes one new traveler, who says, "As a woman my fear of being cooped up in my home without new challenges, new conversations, new vistas far outweighs any fears I might have of traveling solo in a strange land."

Women make 80 percent of all the family travel decisions, so it's not surprising that they finally get around to seeing the world, sometimes by themselves, says Marybeth, a California author, widely quoted travel expert, and consultant.

"I think women are adventurers," says Marybeth. "We have fantasies when we're younger. Maybe we take one adventure trip on a Eurail pass or have a junior year abroad somewhere. Then we have to come home and prove ourselves intellectual beings and plunge into a career. And we have to prove we're a maternal success and have families." Meanwhile, she says, the adventure bug lies dormant.

But at some point, that little girl who spent her Saturday afternoons devouring *National Geographic* magazines realizes it's now time for her to take off. At least for a couple of weeks. "Nothing is as satisfying or as liberating or empowering," says Marybeth, "as walking out that door, away from all that is familiar and safe. It shakes things up. Travel is one of the most powerful ways to change and get back to that little-girl adventurer."

When she appeared on the *Oprah* show, Marybeth said, "For those who think that middle-aged women who travel are looking for a man, let me tell you something: we are looking for ourselves. There is a time when you need to stay home and be a mom and pay attention to a career. And then a time to create, to change your life," she says. "I think women are more willing than men to change because we're used to it. It's also now a time to reconnect with friends. Half of your life is now lived. Who do you really care about? Take a trip with your oldest friends."

As for the safety risks to women traveling alone, Marybeth says, "Fear is healthy. We're taught to be cautious. But then when you hear what other women have done, you think, 'If she can do it and she's not an Amazon, I can. Plus, she's older than I am.'"

Women are not finicky travelers, she says. "We're more accustomed to being spontaneous, to dealing with what doesn't work. We can handle delays and be patient and not consider it a setback." In her travel books she writes about women traveling solo, with daughters, with best friends, and meeting up with traveling companions along the way. "Women connect easily. We start conversations, invite each other to go to dinner." Marybeth, traveling alone, met a Swiss woman on a plane to Delhi and the two ended up renting a houseboat together in Kashmir.

For women who yearn to travel alone but need to get their feet wet, Marybeth advises first going on an organized group trip. "But then at the end of the trip, don't leave with the group. Stay a couple of days by yourself when you're feeling confident about a place. And you'll say, 'Oh my gosh, I can do this.'

"When everyone goes back to the hotel to change for dinner, take a walk alone. Write in your journal. If you're sitting at a café alone, you smell the coffee when you may have forgotten how good coffee smells. You feel the sun on your bare legs. You hear the click of stilettos on cobblestones. If you were with someone else you might not notice."

Be not afraid, says Marybeth. "It's okay if it's scary and you don't speak the language. We all have our own little fiefdoms in our lives where everything works. It's exciting to get outside of that."

Probably one reason that people listen to Marybeth is that she's typical. She is not the kind of woman who buys and renovates the perfect European villa. She's in her fifties and has two teenagers at home, a husband she loves, and parents she's looking after. "It's as hard for me to get away as anyone, but I make it happen."

A Nice Apartment or a Suitcase?

Travel is also an effective way to discover ethnicities, cultures, standards of living, and women's statuses that are different from our own, and to pick up a little humility.

When Mary Goulding was in her seventies she gave up her San Francisco apartment, with its view of the bay, gave away her furniture, and set off for the world. She said she could afford to either continue to rent her lovely apartment or spend her money on travel.

Mary and her late husband, Robert Goulding, were psychotherapists who wrote books and taught at workshops around the world. After Robert died Mary continued to teach. But at seventy-seven she decided "to do something for me," even though she has diabetes and the world had become a scarier place since 9/11.

"My family had a fit. Some of my friends thought I'd lost it," says Mary. In her Christmas letter announcing her decision, she wrote, "As a child it mystified me that in every Oz book

Dorothy wanted to return to Kansas when her adventures were so exciting." The first year she was gone she made it to fifteen countries and spent about $2,000 more than what she normally would in one year in San Francisco on rent and restaurants.

Mary says the advantage of traveling solo is that "people are always eager to practice their English and they'll approach you if you're alone. Then you hear about their lives and views."

Before she left, she put her papers in storage, acquired a post office box in the town where her daughter lives, and sent her books to friends as Christmas presents. She had some concern about what might happen to her if she had a medical emergency during her travels, and she did suffer two broken hips and a small stroke. But she kept traveling, slowed down only slightly by a walker, and celebrated her eightieth birthday by completing a book about her adventures, *Explore the World Alone*.

Who Needs the Big Time?

Mollie shaved her head to play the lead in a production of *Wit*, staged by her repertory theater company in Northern California. "Vivian was a fascinating woman," Mollie says of the lead character, an English professor who has ovarian cancer and is in a hospital receiving experimental chemo. "She's the famous researcher who becomes the one experimented on. She was tough and I admired that, but when I could stand back and look at her, I thought she was very sad. She gave everything to her job and had no other life. No friends came to see her in the hospital. All she had was herself and her thoughts."

Mollie played that character most of one summer in repertory performances, keeping her head shaved and tan, befuddling onlookers as she walked to work in a dress and uncovered bald head. "One street guy called me a transvestite." Her grandson, who had always said he was afraid

FEELING GROOVY?

You don't need a partner. You don't need a ballroom. You don't need special shoes. You certainly don't need an audience. Dancing by yourself not only is good exercise but also releases endorphins that make your innards grin, get your spirit moving, take away stress, and make you grateful to be spinning along with the planet. It creates what some used to refer to as a "natural high." If they could bottle it they would call it an antiaging serum, because it makes your skin glow and your bones happy.

of bald people, ended up asking to have his own head shaved to match Mollie's.

It was a disturbing season, as far as characters go. After *Wit,* Mollie directed *Our Town,* which poignantly explores the mundane and the spiritual aspects of life and death. It was that same year that Mollie's mother died. "It didn't make me fear death, [but] maybe make me understand it more. In *Our Town* none of the characters were ready to die or had any idea they would. Little Wally dies of a burst appendix. Emily dies in childbirth."

For a change of pace, the following season Mollie went zany and played the rehearsal pianist in *The Full Monty.* "This woman has been around. I love her because nothing gets her down. She's been married eight times. She's fun." The role she one day hopes to play is Gertrude in *Hamlet.* "She's about my age, extremely sexy, and she has a zest."

She would have liked to play the young Juliet, who, she says, is "sexy, lots of guts, spunky," although she did once create her as a middle-aged woman in a one-woman play. It was a way for Mollie to deal with her own aging. "What is really sad is when you realize you are too old to play someone and you have to kick them off your list." Her Juliet is fifty and waiting for her lover. She says, "If love be blind, it best agrees with night."

Mollie says the theater gives a person more lives than most. "If I just lived as me it would be really boring. There's not enough time in life to discover a lot."

She started doing theater as a teenager in Seattle, went to Ashland to do bit parts in Oregon Shakespeare Festival productions, and moved to Los Angeles to try to go big time. She decided Hollywood was "a meat market," but she met her husband, who was there trying to become a famous country-and-western singer.

Mollie packed up her notions of making it big in Hollywood or on Broadway and moved with her husband to rural Northern California to raise two boys, dogs, and goats, and help form a local theater company. Her husband drove a truck. Now she helps run the repertory theater, where she often directs, acts, takes tickets, writes songs, and paints sets, all for the same show.

Sometimes she lives her theater roles so thoroughly that she has to warn her husband to ignore her. "When I was doing *Dangerous Liaisons* I told him I was having a hard time dropping Marquise de Merteuil and he'd be better off not taking anything I said too personal."

When she can't sleep she gets up in the dark of night and paints her character's emotions. Or sometimes she works on a novel or a children's story. For more inspiration she dances around her house to the music of Annie Lennox, or Beethoven's "Ode to Joy."

GOT RHYTHM?

Here're some songs that make me and some friends feel like dancing and, of course, singing along, even if we're just sitting at our desk or waiting for the light to change. Try them in your living room. Think of them as *Tomato Tunes*.

- American Woman—Lenny Kravitz
- Cecilia—Simon and Garfunkel
- Crazy Love—Van Morrison
- Dancing Queen—Abba
- Feeding Frenzy—Jimmy Buffett
- Gimme Shelter—Rolling Stones
- Hey Girl—Michael McDonald
- Hey Ya!—Outkast
- Love Shack—B-52's
- Lucky Star—Madonna
- Old Time Rock & Roll—Bob Seger
- Papa's Got a Brand New Bag—James Brown
- Proud Mary—Tina Turner
- Sangue de Beirona—Cesaria Evora

What More Can She Want?

Does this sound familiar? Ellen Boneparth didn't go to law school at Stanford, because she didn't want to compete with her law-student husband. Instead she got a Ph.D. in political science. The marriage ended anyway. And while Ellen says that deferring to her husband was "one of those decisions made without feminist consciousness," the political science detour did lead to a pretty enviable career.

Ellen has been an academic, a writer, and a diplomat. She's lived in Greece, Hawaii, and California. In her late fifties she took a job in Washington DC, because, she says, "how can you read the *New York Times* every morning and not want to try to effect some change in the world?"

Brainy and impish, if one can be described so and still look like Vanessa Redgrave, Ellen is an example of how confidence and credentials can take a woman through many powerful positions, even if she started out not wanting to appear smarter than her man.

In the 1970s Ellen directed a women's studies program at San Jose State University, at a time when such an endeavor was considered near revolutionary. It was an exciting time for women, "when we were being intellectually so turned on by possibilities."

Ellen combined her knowledge and experience with travel, politics, and women in the 1980s and organized an international travel program in women's studies at San Jose State that continues today. "For me it's been this rare opportunity to discover women from a wide variety of backgrounds and develop sisterhood in other countries.

She also went to work for the U.S. Foreign Service, motivated by a desire "to live overseas in a way where people would take me seriously and not consider me just another expat." She had two diplomatic posts, one in Greece and one with the United Nations, and she enjoyed both positions, except for the constraints of working for the government. "Diplomats speak the party line, and I had come out of academia, where I was used to arguing ideas and confronting

216

authority. I became known as a troublemaker and being too outspoken." She also tried going to work one day in burgundy leather pants and, after drawing a number of comments such as "Where did you put your whip and chains?" concluded that "one dare not step out of uniform."

At one time she thought she might want to become a college president, "but I learned that dean is as high as you should go if you want to still be an educator." She also considered running for office, "but I was single and having a great time and I couldn't imagine giving up my fun. "I'm a very restless person, the kind who thinks the grass is always greener. I could not have stayed in one career. I've made a lot of mistakes, but to me, that's better than making just one mistake."

For a time she retired to Greece with her husband to build a house and write books. But after five years she felt too isolated, "and the truth is I didn't become a published author." In her last regular job she was the director of policy and programs for the National Council of Women's Organizations, where she was proudest to be working with young women, "the next group of feminist leaders."

She never had children, but she has a Greek goddaughter she dotes on, and she's mentored several young women. "We have an incredible generation of younger women. I haven't met a one who is not light-years ahead of us at their age. I think part of it is they don't have to go first to a consciousness-raising group to understand their identity as a woman."

At sixty, Ellen says, "The world is still my oyster and I can do whatever I want." She writes an online column that combines travel and women's issues, continues to lead women's studies trips, and gets involved with whatever she decides needs her help, be it gun control or women's rights in Iraq.

Ellen says she doesn't worry about age putting restraints on her next incarnation. "I think it's more about health than how old you are. As long as the body parts all continue to work, I may have to work through many more careers. I still want to save the world."

After a lifetime of saying yes when you don't have the will or the time, and then regretting it, you advance to where you figure out how to say no in a friendly, firm, guilt-free manner. It's either that or say something like "I'm moving to Calcutta in the morning and not taking my cell phone."

This is the script Barbara the banker uses to kindly decline an impossible offer to give of her time when she has none left to give:

"I love your organization and I would love to serve, but I need to keep my promises to the other organizations that I said yes to and feel passionate about. Tell me what kind of skills you're looking for and maybe I can recommend someone."

Keeping a Balance

It wasn't until bank president Barbara Branic entered her fifties that she figured out how to balance her life. "You have to put the big rocks in first. Put the personal stuff on your schedule, time with your husband, your son's graduation. Put those in before the all-important meeting or the community thing."

She learned this from an executive coach she had hired to work with her administrative team, and who helped Barbara learn how to say no. "As a woman you always want to say yes to everything. 'Oh, you want me for your board, how nice.' But then you look around and say, 'This doesn't make sense. I don't have time.'

"I need some introvert time," she says. "It feeds my soul. I try very hard to disappear for at least part of the weekend. To hide, go home, have a glass of wine and watch a video."

As bank president of a regional group, overseeing forty branches and three hundred employees, she says, "It takes a level of intensity, but wishing the level will die down is stupid. It's like wishing life would slow down." Much of her job involves being the public face of her bank and doing work in the community to promote the idea that "what we do really helps people. It's what fires me up every day to put on my pantyhose."

The Storyteller

Holly Near's approach to music, age, and activism is as poetic as any of her songs. "I hold my life with more grace today than I did yesterday." It's not that she suddenly learned something new in her fifties. "It is as if I know the same things I knew thirty years ago but I know them differently. Like yoga, one can learn the poses but it is over time that one improves them, strengthens them, and discovers a more useful way to experience them," she says. Her voice has strengthened, she thinks, as she's gotten older. "My vocal sound is deeper, perhaps has more wood and less glass. I have less vocal strain."

A musician, teacher, and activist, Holly says her basic music style has not changed through the years. "I am a storyteller. I invite the songs to work as a camera lens, [with] close-ups and long views, so that we can experience the small personal details as well as the larger global perspectives, all in a few minutes' time."

Holly's role models in the music world include Nancy Wilson, whom she calls a "jazz vocalist extraordinaire," and all those singers a generation before who really taught her how to sing—Edith Piaf, Judy Garland, Odetta, Ronnie Gilbert, Leontyne Price, Lena Horne, Peggy Lee, Mary Martin, Patsy Cline. "After growing up on those teachers, then all I had to do was figure out what to sing about!"

As to whether music makers tend to keep going longer than others, Holly says, "I'm not sure that musicians are any more vibrant than a nonmusician except for this: when one continues to believe in something, continues to tap into creativity and faith and awe and fascination, then one retains health and hope.

"If a person who is not a musician can tap into this through some other form, then they too carry on. Musicians have the good fortune of knowing where to find connection through their instrument." At middle age, Holly says the work that is of most interest to her is "to learn more about who we are in this world and then to pass on the skills of critical thinking, the passion of activism, the craft of powerful presentation, the art of healing, the humor required to carry on in difficult times, the discipline of active noticing, the courage of telling the truth."

What comes next? "I learn, I pass it on. I learn, I pass it on. How that takes shape in the future, I never know. It is always wide open. I am fortunate that my friends are social change activists rather than cynics. They are my hope genies. I am so glad that I learned early on that activism and service are essential to my sanity. My parents suggested it might be better to live one's life with fascination rather than fear. This has been most useful.

"And when I can't stand the world I let myself rage and weep and put the pillow over my head. And then I get up and remind myself that we are on a planet that is spinning through space at an unimaginable rate of speed and we get to be here, even for a moment. And from that, I take energy."

Sing Until You Drop

In one of her songs Rosalie Sorrels talks about moving to the mountains to dance with the bears, although on the frigid February day we spoke she was doing more freezing than dancing, waiting for the furnace repairman to come because the heat had gone out in her Grimes Creek, Idaho, log cabin. If he didn't come soon she'd have to go out in the snow and chop firewood. No wonder the fans who grew up with Rosalie's songs and stories call her "one ballsy woman."

She's been singing since the 1960s, when she left an abusive husband in Salt Lake City and drove away with five kids back home to Boise. Singing, she says, "was the only way I knew how to make a living," and "it paid more than being a waitress in a truck stop."

Twenty albums, three books, and umpteen awards later, with a schedule that includes performing at the Kennedy Center as well as teaching songwriting in Alaska, she proudly says she's never taken a "day gig," never worked a regular job.

Attitude helped. "I was always pretty sure of myself as a human being and I didn't put up with much. I didn't have to deal with club owners wanting to get laid. They were afraid of me. I had five kids and I'd look at a club owner with the same look I gave my kids—the one that made them say, 'Better not make her mad.'"

She considered all performing jobs. "I never depended on being a folk singer. I played big and small venues. With big and small bands. I sang for everyone who wanted me to sing with them—in prisons, mental hospitals."

Singers are survivors, she says. "Most of the people I admire sang until they dropped. Malvina Reynolds died at seventy-seven and she had gigs still on her calendar."

Rosalie plans to do the same. "Singing is not work to me, it's my life. To stay alive you have to go on doing it." Malvina Reynolds's photo is displayed along with others on Rosalie's "hero ceiling" above her bed—a gallery of faces that include Mercedes Sosa, Bonnie Raitt, Arlo Guthrie, Pete Seeger, and Hunter Thompson.

Rosalie was nominated for her first Grammy at age seventy-one. She didn't win, but she did go to Hollywood for

LET'S NOT FORGET

Others who still have the juice, like:

- Joan Baez
- Emmylou Harris
- Carole King
- Patti LaBelle
- Annie Lennox
- Reba McEntire
- Rita Moreno
- Jessye Norman
- Bonnie Raitt
- Carly Simon
- Barbra Streisand

And vintage storytellers:

- Margaret Atwood
- Louise Erdrich
- Lynn Freed
- Alice Hoffman
- Isabel Allende
- Annie Lamott
- Terry McMillan
- Sue Miller
- Amy Tan
- Alice Walker

the awards show, received a medallion for being a nominee, and hit all the parties. "Except the last one I was really too tired for. That aggravated me. How could I miss a party?"

Rosalie's had her share of misfortune. She lost a son to suicide. Another son went to prison. In her fifties Rosalie had a brain aneurism. "I think people were shocked I lived through that one. But it made me madder than a boiled owl and I learned to walk again in a year. It was accomplished out of a perfect fury. I was fifty-five. I had to make a living. I told myself I don't have time to be sick. That's always been my response to feeling sick. I drink a whole lot of water, eat little, and sleep a lot and say, 'Okay, you can't be sick anymore.'

"I love my life. But at my age I know I don't have much time to fool around. I have to decide what I can do physically. I'm old enough to choose the things that are the most important and then do the best job I can with that. Nothing half-assed. I can't do everything, but whatever I do I want it to mean something."

Some of that philosophy is expressed in her CD *My Last Go Round*. The title is a rodeo term that doesn't mean the last ride, but instead "the best and hardest ride," she says. "It's the ride when all the amateurs have gone home and there's no one left but the pros. It means when you get to that part you do the best work you can muster."

Pretty Good for an Old Hippie

Some say the legs last forever, but Judy Collins insists it's the voice. "That voice muscle lasts the longest, that is, if you don't wreck it, with smoking, screaming, or bad technique," says the folksinger and writer. After saying that and downing a diet cola, she went out on stage and proved it, in that angelic voice. The event was a taping of the public radio show *West Coast Live,* and she performed that night before an audience that was equal parts baby

222

boomers and aging hippies, longtime sing-along fans of this woman who has been celebrating their generation since the 1960s.

Judy Collins held forth without musical backup and her slim beauty took the spotlight without makeup. At sixty-six, the long hair is now piled on her head and white blonde. The eyes are as wide and blue as they were when Steven Stills sang "Suite: Judy Blue Eyes."

Singing is something you can do "until you fall over," she said in a backstage interview. "I think we were created with a voice that can last so we could still cry out from the cave, 'Time for dinner.'"

The singer, author, painter, and activist has had a life with as many highs and lows as her trademark singing range. Her only child committed suicide when he was thirty-two. Judy almost lost her own life and voice to booze. She's dealt with divorce, depression, hepatitis, and TB and written about all of it.

In 1996, she married her longtime partner, Louis Nelson, an industrial designer, in a church wedding in Manhattan. "Pretty good for an old hippie," she says. She continues to do more than thirty shows a year, produce new CDs on her own record label, write books, speak on suicide prevention, and serve as a representative for UNICEF.

"I've never been happier in my life than I am now," she says. "I never felt authentic before these last few years. I guess I'm a slow study in that way, a late bloomer. I never wanted to be anything else but an artist. I've had many years in the saddle and I'm totally joyful when I'm working." Asked whether she pines for that younger voice and pale face with dark hair parted in the middle, she answers, "No, I think we keep growing into ourselves. I'm glad I don't have that voice anymore. That voice is so dark and unexplored, at least in the early years. In later years it starts to lighten up and to grow."

She says, "I've never worried about age, but I do try to look as good as I can. I take my fistful of vitamin pills every day. I exercise every day. I get on the treadmill. I stay fit when I'm on the road." The endorphins she gets from exercise make her happier, she claims, than any drug she ever tried.

She also gets energy from taking a stand, speaking up, and writing songs about real events—the siege in Sarajevo, New York after September 11. "It's my natural state. My whole family is like that. We were raised to be involved."

Boomer Grams

Roughly one-third of today's grandparents are boomers. More than a third of boomers are grandparents. It is expected that by 2010 there will be 80 million American grandparents who will be doing the top five things that grandparents do with their grandkids: eating, watching TV, staying overnight, shopping for clothes, and playing. The activities sound pretty standard, but the numbers mean a growing group of consumers wanting to spend money on books and toys and those adorable doll-like outfits that no parent in her right mind would put on her credit card. The consumer figures, reported on www.igrandparents.com, show that one out of every four toys sold in America is purchased by a grandparent. Marketers are mindful of the growing number of boomer grandparents and are pushing adventure travel and computer camps for grandparents and grandkids to experience together, special grandparent/grandkid menus, and discounts to theme parks and movie theaters.

I'm not sure if making a worm house in the backyard fits into a consumer category, but that's what Penny does when she goes to Austin, Texas, to be with her grandkids. As a soccer-playing grandma she spends time coaching the grandkids and volunteering at their preschool. With her other grandkids in California she looks for crows and hawks and visits a butterfly farm. Against her better judgment she also plays Barbies with one granddaughter ("I'm gagging," she says) and sews doll clothes.

224

With research showing that parenting is good for mental lethargy, there's enticement for grandparents to continue the fun and games with their grandkids. For boomers wanting to stay hooked into the world of youth, what better liaison than a grandchild?

Neva, who has two grandkids in Boulder, Colorado, likes watching the evolutionary process. "I had a childhood that wasn't that great, and I took the parts that were positive and moved on into my new world. I tried to give to my son and stepdaughter the best of what was in me. My stepdaughter is the most wonderful mother. I see evolution in grand measure in those grandbabies, and I am trying to be the most excellent 'Ama' possible in the presence of such magnificence. We greet each other with great shouts and tears of joy and dance down the airport runway together."

Emmie is another frequent-flier grandma. One grandchild is in Colorado and two are in California. Before the babies were born she and her daughter used to spend their visits staying up late and talking, discovering new restaurants, going to museums. "Now our schedule is totally different. Since we take the twin babies with us most of the time, it is hard to have a leisurely lunch, and dinner is usually takeout that we eat at home after the babies go to bed. We nap when the babies nap so we can keep up. We are too tired to make it all the way through a movie video so we usually watch it over two

AND THE MUSIC GOES ON AND ON

You think about those sounds that stay in your head, the ones that soothe you when you're blue, that stir you to shake your hips, and even urge you into the street for certain causes, and you have to be grateful that these music makers keep pumping it out.

Think of all those women who broke into the boys' club of pop music in the 1960s and 1970s, the ones whose voices carry on along with us—Tina, Aretha, Joni, Judy, Barbra, Rosalie, Bonnie, Carole, Linda, Holly.

REMEMBERING JANIS

Like many heavenly voiced and messed-up 1960s stars, Janis Joplin never got to grow old. If she had lived as long as her fans, she'd be in her sixties. Her long brown hair would be shot with gray, or she might have added owl feathers. She might be one of those vintage mamas you see with tattoos on their breasts, flower children old enough to be grandmothers. She would have been fun to have around.

I was playing some good old Janis tunes one afternoon while painting the living room, wailing along to "Cry Baby." My husband poked his head in the door and asked if I'd hurt myself. Using my best off-key alto, I sang out, "All you ever gotta do is be a good man one time to one woman."

to three nights." But she also gushes appropriately. "Babies are so much fun to watch develop their personalities, learn to walk, start talking."

"The biggest surprise for me about becoming a grandmother was that I like it so much," says Judy. Her grandchildren live in Virginia, she in Massachusetts. "If I were close geographically and had to deal with babysitting requests, I'd have to keep that at a minimum. I know I don't want to be a babysitting grandmother, although I'm thrilled to know these babies and watch them grow. There's an undefinable wonderful something about experiencing my own children's children and watching my child interact with his child, deal with problems. I think I'm like my grandmother in that I like to provide warmth and succor to the children and to somehow ease their experience of the world."

Salli sees herself as striving to "embellish and spritz up as much of life as possible" for her grandkids. She was surprised at "how seductive it is to have no agenda, to give myself permission to just be. They give me many opportunities to sit and watch the sun move slowly across the hardwood floor and shift sand over and over through my fingers." She actually learned her grandmother skills from a much-older sister. "She wore the apron and provided after-school chocolate chip cookies when I was little. She made Jell-O creations and wacky cakes and served green mashed potatoes on a gray winter day. A grandparent doesn't have to be old. She just has to have a different generation's perspective and not be so invested in having you brush your teeth."

Grandma, What Big Underpants You Have

Terry was dressing when her granddaughter walked into the bedroom, eyed Terry's underwear lying on the bed and said, "Boy, Oma. You wear big underpants."

Taking immediate action, Terry got rid of all of her big underpants and went right out and bought some hipsters. "I would have bought bikini panties but I'd need a full butt lift to wear them again." Still, both Terry's granddaughter and husband were happy with the change.

Do not think that women of a certain age do not care about panty lines. Do not think that we are beyond spending the price of a good bottle of wine on one pair of silk skivvies in a color and style contrary to our persona. I admit, however, to some ambivalence about thongs. Didn't we spend most of our lives making sure we didn't have a "snuggy," only to find out that some women like it that way? It's been trendy for young women to wear them with low-rise jeans, so that the top of the panties is visible from the back. I'm not sure why you want people seeing your underwear, although I do like the little-lace-camisole peekaboo look to soften a tailored jacket.

Many of us who wouldn't have dared venture into Janis's world considered her the best of the bad girls, with her slick jeans and cowboy boots, cleavage and love beads. She had a voice that made you want to get down in the mud or fly with the angels. She died when she was twenty-seven, when many of her generation were hurrying to have babies and balance marriage with careers. She didn't get to have kids, long for a house in Italy, or have a midlife crisis.

She's been gone so long that her contemporaries are starting to consider early retirement and study Elderhostel brochures. But when I listen to Janis I don't think of an icon. I think of her as a hippie chick and when I blast her music my inner hippie chick lets loose and sings out, "You gotta get it while you can."

In aerobics class one day I happened to notice that our instructor seemed to have a free-floating waistband showing above her tights. Could it be a thong? I asked. It was, she said, setting off a discussion about the merits of such. What's so great about having something in your butt? we inquired indelicately. No panty line, she said. Then why wear anything at all? we asked. Try it—you'll like it, she advised.

Not wanting to appear closed minded I talked a friend into going thong shopping. Picking through the sale bins at a high-priced boutique we giggled like teenagers buying our first 28 AA bras.

One fun thing about wearing thong underwear, I discovered, is the response you get from a man who is accustomed to seeing you in what I believe are called French-cut briefs. In your first thong appearance, "What the hell is that?" is not what you hope to hear. One would rather the response be, "Come here, you global wonder." Author Diane Johnson writes that a French woman's sexy lingerie is an indicator of self-indulgence and self-respect.

We need to get rid of the ratty stuff. Throw out all old underwear. Including anything with tired elastic and a faded color from being washed too many times. If you ever find yourself wondering, "What is my mother's bra doing in my laundry basket?" it's time to go see what's new at the lingerie shop. You might also want to buy something with a better fit.

Fashion consultant Brenda Kinsel says women often stick to the same old bra size "as if it were nonnegotiable, like the color of their eyes." Fit is everything. "If you're in underwear that is sized right, you really shouldn't notice it in the day nor should anyone else following from the back notice it either. Too-tight underwear is noticed. That's where you get the double butt effect; there's the smile line of your butt and then there's the smile line a few inches higher from your underwear."

Brenda does lots of underwear shopping with her clients to find just the right fit in bras "and to find those undergarments that make the outer garments look better." An underwear splurge, she said, is much more important than purchasing an additional pair of shoes.

And there's the lusciousness of it all. Even if the only person who sees you in your undies is your cat, having something that caresses your skin is a sweet luxury that we deserve now more than ever. Besides, when those airport security guards search your carry-on, they'll pull out something more eye popping than grandma pants.

Here's another underwear-related irony. The same women who once enjoyed going braless are now into them. My friend Sara, who remembers the free-swinging days of Woodstock, now spends $50 on her French bras. (Hey, that's nothing. I know a man who spent almost as much for special motorcycle underwear.) She likes that the bras don't give her a shelf look, show nipples, or reveal back fat. "I used to see these women with tight clothes and large breasts and nothing was bulging anywhere. I think that's what this does. It contours me and smoothes me out. If I could get a bathing suit that has that same shape, I'd pay a lot of money."

Our bodies deserve the best. And it can be your little secret. The world may think you're a plain old blue-jeans kind of gal, but hiding underneath that denim is an $8 tiger-striped G-string that makes you frisky just thinking about it.

MYTH: Middle-aged women can't help but be lumpy and out of shape.
FACT: After a year of twice-a-week strength training, women's fifty-year-old-plus bodies can become fifteen to twenty years more youthful.

MYTH: Technology is for young people.
FACT: Big cop-out. Fifty-one percent of Americans ages fifty to sixty-four have Internet access, as do 15 percent of the sixty-five-and-over population. Sixty-nine percent of them go online every day.

MYTH: I'll never have sex again.
FACT: Seventeen percent of single women ages fifty to fifty-nine told AARP they were having intercourse at least once a week. Fifty percent of married women said the same.

Rewriting the "R" Word

Talking with friends one night at a party, I realized that we had openly been using the "R" word. Without cringing. You know the "R" word. It's the one in AARP. Or, as a skeptical friend says, the R in RV. It's the one that you used to associate with your parents' generation but now can attach to your own. People are bailing out, and they're doing it earlier than you'd expect and in very different ways. An example: a couple from the Midwest swings through town, saying they're scouting places to live when they retire from their jobs. Retire, like stopping work and playing golf? No, they say, retire as in getting away from the snow and telecommuting.

As takeovers, restructuring, buyouts, and downsizing radically remodel the work world, careers are being ended or being redirected with a strong nudge. People a lot younger than sixty-five are calling themselves retired, like the forty-five-year-old who left her job at Silicon Valley and spent the past six months finally getting her house in order after two cross-country job moves. She knows she'll get antsy. "You can't spend every day wiping off your counters." So will she do the traditional thing and move to Florida? No, she said, but she might do some consulting and begin to paint again.

Retirement is one of those love/hate issues. You may relish the idea of having nothing to do, but what if it were your only option? For all our whining about wanting more time, we don't necessarily mean time with an R rating. This, as they say, is not your parents' retirement. This is doing something completely different after years of doing the same thing. Detouring, perhaps. "I think we need to change the name from 'retire' to something else," says a friend who is considering alternatives to working as a publicist. How about "metamorphose" instead? Or "transmute"?

According to an AARP study, 80 percent of boomers plan to work part-time after they retire. A lot of experts agree—that our traditional system in which people work like crazy and then suddenly stop because they've reached some number doesn't make sense. Ken Dychtwald, who writes about the changes boomers are effecting in all aspects of aging, suggests we use our longevity to rotate into several different careers. Instead of having all the work take place during one part of life and all leisure happen during another, mix it up, he says. Get out of one line of work, go to Mexico for a while, then come back and find a brand-new job. He can see people working off and on this way into their eighties.

Dychtwald says that the traditional retirement age was actually established in the 1930s as a way to open up positions for a glut of unemployed young people. That's not the case now. In fact, employers are beginning to wonder what will happen when boomers, who made up at least a third of the workforce in 2005, start retiring in large packs by 2010.

Some say it won't be a problem because boomers are too identified by their work to give it up, and some haven't saved enough to even think of retiring. Emmie in Denver says she'll retire "when I can afford to live like I want to live." Her vision of retirement is "traveling, visiting friends, reading, going to the coffee shop in the morning with the *New York Times*, working out, resuming my painting lessons, managing electronic pictures of my grandchildren, volunteering at the museum or hospital, and trading stocks." Lucky for Emmie, she works for a company that provides retirement plans, so she will know when the time and the money are right.

Having enough money to retire is another issue for long-lived boomers who would face almost thirty years of life on a fixed income were they to retire in their sixties. Eve, a Boston professor, has been fiscally planning for retirement even though there's no set retirement age in her job. "I'm maxing out on the pension system and every kind of insurance that's available to me. I'm very risk averse. My father died in his nineties and my mother is still living in her nineties. I'm going to need a lot of savings."

Joanie talks about easing back on her work in her fifties, "working less, skiing more. I don't want to wait until I'm sixty-five. I think of all the things I might want to do. I hear on the radio about a Vermont farmer writing on his farm and I say to my husband, let's do that. The next day, it's something else.

"I know you could be more affluent if you did keep working, but some people make a decision not to max out. I think about my parents' generation, who used up all their gas working. The breadwinner worked until he crapped out or until someone said, 'We're done with you.' That doesn't sound good either."

And yet, forced retirement built on a notion that everyone has a finite number of valuable working years stops too many talented and energetic people in their tracks. If retiring from one job meant having the freedom to go into something else that rang your bells, particularly if your bells haven't been rung for a while, then it would be something to look forward to. Dychtwald says retirement policies and attitudes are changing, and just in time for us. But that doesn't mean that some people won't still want to retire the old-fashioned way—move to the beach, and buy a metal detector.

HOW AND WHEN?

How do you decide when and how to give up the career, the paycheck, the big city lunches, and, for many women, the professional identity that for much of your life has answered the question, "What do you do?" Homework is required.

The tough part. Money and health are pivotal issues. You need a fair amount of both if you're going to be one of those crinkly-eyed women in the ads walking on the beach and saying every day is Saturday. When those two biggies are in place, you can think about the fun stuff—where you'll live, who with, and what you'll do with your time and energy.

Can you afford it? Find a numbers person to talk to about money. What do you have? What will you need to live on? Most women will need a combo of savings, social security, pensions, and 401(k). If you sell the movie script, inherit a bundle, or win the lottery, that's extra. Talk to a tax consultant or financial advisor. And look around online. wiserwomen.org is one Web site that counsels on retirement and financial planning and helps you ask yourself the tough questions.

What about health insurance? Does your health insurance go with you when you leave the job? Not likely, unless it's part of a sweet buyout or golden parachute. You'll probably have to go shopping. Ask around about group plans, private insurance, and Medicare supplemental plans. If you move, make sure that there's a doctor who takes Medicare in addition to there being good hiking trails.

Are you ready? Traditionally people retire in their early to mid-sixties, but boomers talk about working way beyond, into their seventies and eighties, at least part-time. Eighty percent of boomers plan to work in some form or another after sixty-five, according to the AARP. Already, twice as many Americans seventy-five and over work now as did twenty years ago, says the Bureau of Labor Statistics.

But can you? Do they want you around? With so many boomers approaching retirement age, some employers are getting nervous about brain drain and encouraging older workers to stay on—at least the ones valued for their special skills, expertise, and institutional memory. You might be able to stay on as part-time, flextime, or as a job share. And there's always being a consultant.

What if he's ready and you're not? It's not like the old days when retirement was largely the working man's decision. Now there are often two breadwinners in a household. What's the compromise when she wants to keep going into the office and he's longing to buy a horse farm?

Consider all options. There is no one way to retire. Do you want to live in the wide-open spaces or have neighbors you can count on? Where is the best place for you—the desert or downtown? The census bureau predicts that through 2025 a huge chunk of seniors will be moving to the west, to states like Utah and Wyoming. Check into cohousing, where residents plan the community, own their own units, and share maintenance and sometimes dinner.

Talk it up. Women together can figure it out. New Choices in Seattle, and the Red Shoes in Baton Rouge, mentioned earlier, are examples of local gathering spots for women to counsel each other. Look, too, to www.womansage.com, based in Orange County, California, which provides a salon to talk about retirement options and other midlife issues. Same with the Transition Network, started in New York City for professional women moving from career into the next phase.

We'd Call It Geezer City

Have you had this discussion? "When we aging boomers turn into full-on codgers we'll quit our jobs and buy a place together." "How about we remodel an old motel where a bunch of us live together and keep an eye on each other?" "With room to play music!" "And it'll be a place that needs enough fixing so the handy people among us can build a fence or hoe in the garden." "Maybe we'd be okay with growing old as long as we're using our hands and brains and sitting on the front porch with friends."

Boomers are going to create a huge bulge in the senior population, with life spans nearing ninety and one hundred. The number of people age sixty-five and up is expected to double, to 70.3 million by 2030, according to the U.S. Census Bureau. By 2030 the number of Americans sixty-five and older will account for one in five Americans, say the experts at the Centers for Disease Control and Prevention. California alone expects a 200-percent jump in people eighty-five and up over the next forty years.

This inspires lots of talk about a "longevity revolution" and what it will all mean for health care and Social Security. Will there be enough nursing homes and assisted living centers? Where will these people live? Who will take care of them?

By *them* they mean *us*.

Maybe we want something different than our parents' retirement community. Maybe we don't want to be stuck without a car in the suburbs waiting for the sprinklers to come on. Perhaps we want something a little more tie-dyed. Pool our equity and do a back-to-the-land venture. Build a big old compound and make music, stay up late discussing politics and griping about health care plans. Carpool to Earth Elder events and protest marches. Or find some spot to pull all our trailers in a circle and share a DSL line.

It's not an unusual fantasy. If we don't like the traditional choices, we'll have to come up with something. Terry and her husband and four other couples have been moving to Phoenix, one by one, from different parts of the country, where they'll create their own "Sun City" (she says "Sin City"). Another boomer, an artist, says she and her husband are making plans to move in with a bunch of other artists, since none of them has a 401(k) or pension plan. She imagines them all sharing a cheap live-work space in their burnt-sienna years.

Think of the possibilities. We'd create wonderful libraries with old-fashioned books made out of paper, including first-edition copies of *Catcher in the Rye* and *Our Bodies, Ourselves.* There would be music on vinyl, including the original *White Album.* There'd be no need to set quiet times—with everyone's ears wrecked by a life of listening to rock and roll, it would just be a matter of unplugging your hearing aid if you wanted to go to bed early.

Aging experts say that, due to improved diet, medical care, and exercise, older Americans will live healthier and more vigorously than ever. The challenge, then, will be to do it creatively. Here's a second chance to be a hippie, at seventy-five. We could call ourselves "flower fogies."

Plan Now to Rest in Peace

It's important to have things written down, clear instructions for your exit. Otherwise, mistakes may be made. For example, when my dad died suddenly at our parents' home in Pennsylvania, we didn't know what he would have wanted. Even though he had made many preparations for himself and our mother, we'd never had the big family discussion, and the information wasn't located in an easy-to-find spot. Our lack of information was compounded by the fact that our mother had early Alzheimer's and wasn't able to provide much guidance. If the paperwork wasn't in the safe-deposit box at their bank, she hadn't a clue.

So, when we asked, "Mom, where would Daddy want to be buried?" she said Townville. And when we asked which church would do his funeral, she said the Baptist Church. My sister and I both thought these were odd choices. He was a Methodist and they had never lived in Townville. But our mother was adamant that she knew what Daddy had wanted.

It was only after the funeral and burial that my brother-in-law came across a receipt for two burial plots in a wallet in my father's desk. We thought we had thoroughly gone through that wallet, but we'd somehow missed this important piece of paper, which said they were both to be buried in a cemetery far from Townville. We eventually got the money back for the unused plots and our father's body stayed interred in Townville.

Some time later, we realized the reason for the confusion. When we had asked our mother where "Daddy" would want to be buried, her brain must have conjured the image not of our daddy but of her own (long-dead) father, whom she, too, called "Daddy." He, of course, was already buried in Townville and was indeed a Baptist.

A Living Will Party

Really, it can be fun, or at least satisfying. The subject is dying, but the atmosphere is friendly. You finally get the forms filled out and everyone stops procrastinating. You gather everyone in the living room or around the kitchen table to talk about unpleasant possibilities, and tell denial and discomfort to wait in the closet.

We know what happens if you don't put things in writing. Families disagree. The court steps in. The state steps in. If it gets really nasty our vegetative self ends up on the nightly news, like Terri Schiavo. We don't want busloads of people coming to our hospital bed to argue over whether we live or die. It's just another pesky form to fill out, like applying for a student loan or an equity line. They take time and they're tedious but they're the only way to get what we want. So, we fill out the forms.

They're called Advanced Health Care Directives, sometimes known as "living wills," and they can be procured from medical associations, hospitals, lawyers, and several different Web sites. The forms are designed so that you don't need a lawyer's assistance, but if you happen to have a lawyer or a doctor for a friend, you could invite them to the party. Maybe they haven't filled out theirs either.

The directive does two things. Basically it tells medical people when and when not to use life-sustaining methods in the event you cannot communicate your wishes. It gives a spouse, child, or some other adult the power and responsibility to make decisions for you.

Once you've filled out the forms, and signed them in the presence of witnesses or a notary, you'll need to give a copy to your doctor, your kids, your spouse, and whoever is your health care designate. Then you can sit down with your kids and tell them where you keep the important papers, the advanced directive, your will, the trust if you have one, the map showing the location of the septic tank, the name of your lawyer. You can tell them how you feel about donating your organs. You can make them understand your thoughts about burial or cremation, why you want your ashes scattered in Yosemite and not Machu Picchu, and that all these years you've been secretly keeping a getaway cabin in the Ozarks, which they can now use.

Your kids will say they don't want to talk about it. Tell them it makes you feel better, and, by the way, have they done their personal papers? They could start by throwing a party.

"I've learned that people will forget what you said, people will forget what you did, but people will never forget how you made them feel."
—maya angelou

Change the Ending

Marin County, California, has a burial ground that is part of a nature preserve. Bodies are put in the ground like they were one hundred years ago, without an airtight casket and a cement vault. Embalming is not allowed. Caskets have to be biodegradable. Just like us.

This alternative cemetery is designed for those who "want to feel close to the natural world" but don't want to add to the wasted space of standard cemeteries. Clients buy interment rights that protect the land from being developed and maintain its natural state. The burial plots are marked by a piece of driftwood, special rock, or bush instead of a marble slab or stone angel, and the grounds are laced with hiking trails with views of the Pacific. Picnicking is encouraged.

The guiding philosophy is that once you die you get to be a part of nature and save it at the same time. The Marin model, known as a "green cemetery," was patterned after a burial preserve in rural South Carolina, but the idea of an organic repose is another aspect of the natural death movement pioneered in Northern California in the 1990s.

Northern California is also the home base of Final Passages, an organization that helps families do home funerals. Jerri Lyons of Sebastopol, known by some as a death midwife, offers ideas on alternative funerals, showing families how to bypass expensive funeral plans—laying out Aunt Edith in the living room, and then wrapping her body and delivering it themselves to the crematory or cemetery.

Another alternative to the traditional funeral approach is casket maker Kathleen Broderson's. The Forestville woman designs unadorned pine boxes that customers use as linen chests or book shelves until a family member needs to go into the ground. She learned her building skills from her father and it was for him that she made her first pine box five years ago.

There are many people starting to look at dying and death in different ways. Kate Munger of Inverness, California, directs the Threshold Choir, whose members sing at the bed of the dying throughout the San Francisco Bay Area. Kate discovered this way of using song while caring for a friend with AIDS. She started singing to him and said she knew she'd given him a gift. "And I knew the future of my life was starting." She started with a choir in Marin County and then helped start branches of the choir in several cities in Northern California.

The choir's standards range from "Ave Maria" to Kate Wolf's "Across the Great Divide," but they also do special requests. Kate sang to a woman with Alzheimer's whose daughters thought their mother might enjoy her favorite show tunes. Soon the woman herself was joining in. Before that she hadn't put two words together in months. "In musical language she was not impaired," says Kate, whose model has been repeated in Oregon and Minnesota.

The notion of deinstitutionalizing death is still mostly a California happening, but it's certainly popular. After newspaper stories on the Marin burial grounds appeared, the owners reported a waiting list of seven hundred, mostly boomers, who signed up to get in.

Doris Style

Doris doesn't like to be called a role model. She thinks it sets her apart and she likes being in the thick of things. She certainly doesn't want to be deferred to because of her age. She did, however, allow friends to celebrate her ninety-fifth birthday. It was a fine party, with champagne and chocolate cake at one of her friend's homes, next to a redwood tree said to be six hundred years old. By comparison, ninety-five seems like a mere sapling.

Doris looked regal and held court, but a surprising thing happened to her after that. Everybody started thinking of her as ninety-five. "People say to me, 'You're ninety-five? That's amazing.' I can't stand people being solicitous. Sometimes I want to hit them. But I guess you're supposed to act nice when you're ninety-five."

"Nice" is not a big enough word for Doris. Formidable, keen, passionate, certainly. Definitely frank. These are more accurate descriptors for her.

Doris is a therapist who gave up her practice only five years ago. Maybe it's her professional openness that makes her such a draw, along with her wit, political zeal, fierce loyalty to her community, and shrewd historical perspective. In the last few years Doris has been writing her memoirs, many of them based on her years with her husband, Joe, a controversial labor union leader in San Francisco in the 1930s to 1950s. Her stories are peppered with smoke-filled rooms, late-night clubbing, and political drama, slices of life from their forty-seven years together.

She likes to fill her mountain-top home with people, build a fire, tuck her legs up on the couch, pour a glass of Scotch, and talk into the night. I asked how she manages to have so many friends of different ages. "I like to be with people who have the same interests as I do. A lot of my younger friends and I have been on the same committees. When you're working toward the same goal age makes no difference. I know there are obvious differences in our lives. But they don't treat me any different than if I were sixty. And I have never acted like they should."

A group of women friends who are mostly middle aged often gather at Doris's. We talk about writing, environmental concerns, politics, gossip, men. One afternoon she had us all crying when she read an excerpt from her book about Joe's death and how they had made love the night before he went into surgery. Sometimes the conversation drifts into "girly stuff" like clothes and hair, which prompts Doris to say, "Can we please stop talking about hair and get onto something interesting?"

Not that she doesn't have her own vain moments. No one gets to see her before she has on her makeup and is dressed for the day. She keeps her hair strawberry blonde and admits to having had cosmetic surgery once. "It was a little tuck, to get rid of the lines around my mouth. I was sixty-five, an age when some people think you're supposed to retire. I thought I needed to look younger. I thought if it looked really good, I'd do more cosmetic surgery, but it didn't make that much of a difference. But if anyone I know is tempted, I cheer them on. If you have the money and a good surgeon and it gives you more self-confidence, why not?"

Doris's independence and longevity come from her mother, who lived to be one hundred and who insisted on remaining in her home, despite invitations to move in with family members.

After Doris's husband died she continued to work with therapy clients. "I always loved this field. I knew from college it was what I wanted. I stopped going to the office (a family counseling agency) when I was eighty. Then I had an office at the health center and didn't really retire until I was ninety. It was satisfying, so why would I quit? If your brain is still working, you can be a therapist. And you get better the more you do it."

She's also been a tireless community organizer in her town of Occidental, California, putting together a community council that developed programs that provided low-cost lunches and volunteer rides for seniors, and created a performing arts center. The latter is Doris's latest brainchild. "Musicians complained about only having the church to play in, and I said, why can't we just build a place where we can have concerts?" After much fund-raising and politicking, Occidental got its arts center.

"I feel good that everything I've started has materialized. I know some people disagree with how I do things. There were old-timers who didn't like me butting in. Now, most of us are friends. I do it because I love this town." Her house sits on a hill above Occidental, surrounded by redwood trees and rhododendron bushes. She scoffs at suggestions that she move closer to the town. "I like the trees and the quiet. Joe and I built this. It's my home and still part of him."

Doris has outlived many friends and maintained her health longer than most of her contemporaries, although she did have breast cancer twice, the first time when she was sixty-nine and the second at eighty-five. "Joe was still alive when I had my first one. He said the nicest thing. He said not to worry; he'd give all his attention to my other breast."

At her birthday party someone asked Doris if she had any regrets. She declined to state, saying all of her life was good, even the sad times. When we talked privately, she spoke of one regret involving a girlhood friend. Doris and the woman had kept in touch through the years but had little in common. "She was often depressed, very moody. Now I know she was probably bipolar. She came to visit us once and I think I was kind of mean to her. The year we were both sixty-five, her second husband died. She called and asked if I would come visit, and I said I couldn't travel right then. Soon after that, she committed suicide. I should have recognized the depth of her depression. I think that's what you regret the most, if you've been unkind to someone."

Back on the subject of age, she says, "I think of myself as the same person I've always been. I kept getting older without thinking about it. Then, suddenly I was ninety-five years old. I guess because I can't see and I can't walk well my body gives me away. People see me as old. But do I have to behave like I'm ninety-five? Now everybody wants to wait on me. They assume I need things. I don't have any problem asking for another drink if I want one. Maybe when I'm ninety-six people will stop paying attention to my age."

HEIRLOOM TOMATOES

They are the classic ones, the classy dames who held their own as long as they were around. The long-gone ones you would have liked to meet on a rainy night when you were both waiting for a cab and started talking.

Here are some of my favorites. You add yours.

Julia Child, the cooking diva who loved red meat and gin and, when asked what would she have done with her life had she not devoted it to food, said, "I would have probably married some Republican banker and become an alcoholic."

Anne Bancroft, whom Arthur Penn directed twice on Broadway. "More happens in her face in ten seconds than happens in most women's faces in ten years," he said.

Lillian Hellman, who stopped writing plays in her late fifties and then started writing books and was said to have propositioned a young dinner companion when she was seventy-nine.

M. F. K. Fisher, who wrote seductively of food and life and said, "So it happens that when I write of hunger, I am really writing about love and the hunger for it, and warmth and the love of it and the hunger for it."

Freya Stark, who took off on her own to explore and write about the world, starting with Lebanon to learn Arabic, and who lived to be one hundred, with more stories left to tell.

Shirley Chisholm, the first black woman elected to Congress, who said her greatest political asset, "which professional politicians fear, is my mouth, out of which come all kinds of things one shouldn't always discuss for reasons of political expediency."

"The great thing about getting older is that you don't lose all the other ages you've been." —madeleine l'engle

A Toast to All Tomatoes

Good health, a sharp mind, a young spine, loyal friends, an adoring family, survivable income, a clear mammogram, an open heart to a world in need, and a lover who thinks you're the hottest creature around . . . except for maybe Susan Sarandon.

WHERE TO GO FROM HERE

With all the great women around us and new ones to meet, there will be no end to the good and true companions you'll find in your next chapter. But if you need backup, here are sites and sources from some of the Tomatoes you met inside.

Authors and Sources
- Paula Begoun — **www.cosmeticscop.com**
- Meredith Blevins — **www.meredithblevins.com**
- Marybeth Bond — **www.gutsytraveler.com**
- Ellen Boneparth — **www.openroad.openmind.com**
- Brenda Kinsel — **www.brendakinsel.com**
- Joan Price — **www.joanprice.com**

Health Sites
- Alzheimer's Association — **www.alz.org**
- American Heart Association — **www.americanheart.org**
- American Stroke Association — **www.strokeassociation.org**
- Office of the U.S. Surgeon General — **www.surgeongeneral.gov**
- Society for Women's Health Research — **www.womenshealthresearch.org**
- Women's Health Initiative — **www.whi.org**